D1574739

MOTIVATION

Stefan Falk is an internationally recognized executive coach and human performance expert. A McKinsey & Company alumnus specializing in leadership and corporate transformation, he has trained over 4,000 leaders across more than sixty different client organizations in North America and Europe. He has held C-suite roles at several global companies, and has been responsible for driving corporate transformations valued in excess of two billion dollars. His leadership and human performance techniques have been developed in continuous cooperation with leading scientists in fields including neuroscience, behavioral science, and psychology. He is the author of *Motivation* (known as *Intrinsic Motivation* in America) and the co-author of *Neuroleadership*.

MOTIVATION

HOW TO LOVE
YOUR WORK
AND SUCCEED AS
NEVER BEFORE

STEFAN FALK

MACMILLAN

First published 2022 by St. Martin's Press,
an imprint of St Martin's Publishing Group

First published in the UK 2023 by Macmillan
an imprint of Pan Macmillan
The Smithson, 6 Briset Street, London EC1M 5NR
EU representative: Macmillan Publishers Ireland Ltd, 1st Floor,
The Liffey Trust Centre, 117–126 Sheriff Street Upper,
Dublin 1, D01 YC43
Associated companies throughout the world
www.panmacmillan.com

ISBN: 978-1-0350-1698-3 HB
ISBN: 978-1-0350-1699-0 TPB

Copyright © Stefan Falk 2022

The right of Stefan Falk to be identified as the
author of this work has been asserted by him in accordance
with the Copyright, Designs and Patents Act 1988.

All rights reserved. No part of this publication may be reproduced,
stored in a retrieval system, or transmitted, in any form, or by any means
(electronic, mechanical, photocopying, recording or otherwise)
without the prior written permission of the publisher.

Pan Macmillan does not have any control over, or any responsibility for,
any author or third-party websites referred to in or on this book.

1 3 5 7 9 8 6 4 2

A CIP catalogue record for this book is available from the British Library.

Printed and bound by CPI Group (UK) Ltd, Croydon, CR0 4YY

This book is sold subject to the condition that it shall not, by way of
trade or otherwise, be lent, hired out, or otherwise circulated without
the publisher's prior consent in any form of binding or cover other than
that in which it is published and without a similar condition including
this condition being imposed on the subsequent purchaser.

Visit **www.panmacmillan.com** to read more about all our books
and to buy them. You will also find features, author interviews and
news of any author events, and you can sign up for e-newsletters
so that you're always first to hear about our new releases.

Dedicated to Geddy Lee, Alex Lifeson,
Neil Peart, Ian Paice, Jon Lord, Roger Glover,
Ritchie Blackmore, Ian Gillan, David Bowie,
Zeb Macahan; the love of my life, Regina;
and my son, Ramses

*Always be yourself unless you can be Hanuman,
then always be Hanuman.*

Contents

Section Two:
Shape Your Destiny:
Evolve Your Mindset to Become the Superstar You Can Be

Section Three:
Master the Second-Biggest Obstacle for
Professional Success and Well-Being: Other People

Acknowledgments

It is virtually impossible to write an acknowledgment that fully describes what has made this book possible. So many moments, so many people, have contributed to it. Obviously, I owe a huge debt of thanks to all the thousands of people I have worked with—colleagues, direct reports, and clients. By inviting me to help you with your challenges, all of you have offered me opportunities to learn and grow, and by that you have all contributed to this book.

But I am also grateful for what I view as one of the most important things in life: all of my *own* challenges, hardships, and failures, especially as a little overweight kid with no friends and a father who scared me stiff. I am thankful for all the people who have challenged me over the years, even those who tried to set me up for failure or tried to hurt me in other ways. All of that has made me a stronger, more self-aware person who thrives on taking on the impossible (which I have repeatedly learned nothing is). These personal qualities have contributed to the choices I have made personally and professionally. They have also enabled me to develop what has been completely decisive for all my activities and adventures in life, including my coaching practice and the contents of this book: a focused but creative brain, which lives its own life.

My brain has an amazing ability to project the future and

envision any end state, whether it is clients becoming the best at what they do or me taking on a completely new area I am clueless about but nonetheless succeeding at. My brain always comes up with a road map for reaching a good outcome. It is almost as if there is no problem related to my own or other people's dreams, performance, mental well-being, and success my brain can't crack.

One person's decision has been extremely important for my being able to write this book. For some reason that I still can't completely understand, my mom made up her mind to rent me a piano when I was eight. We had not talked about me playing a musical instrument before. Maybe she'd noticed how much I enjoyed it when my uncle sang and played the guitar for me, or how much I liked to play her records—I can still remember playing Lynn Anderson's "(I Never Promised You A) Rose Garden" and Elvis's "Love Me Tender" repeatedly. Playing the piano made me realize at an early age that the activity itself does not matter; it is how you think about it that makes you love it or not. This is the basic premise of not only this book but my entire life.

When I got older, three people contributed even more to who I am, what I do, and the tools and principles of this book. My mentor for many years, Mihaly Csikszentmihalyi, who passed in 2021, played an extremely important role in my life. What Mihaly did not know about the human condition, how we evolve, and what makes human existence a blessing is not worth knowing. Mihaly was a true scientist, meticulous about backing up all his insights with facts and research. His intelligence and ability to see things clearly were never intimidating, but could be irritating at times, especially when I thought I had come up with something "really smart," only to realize that he had already thought of it. Anyone who wants to evolve and get as much out of life as possible should read Mihaly's work.

Another person who played an important role for me is John Douglas, the former FBI agent and a pioneer in criminal profiling. The first time we met, he showed me crime-scene photos, analyzing each scene and telling me what he saw in them that revealed the perpetrators' motives and behavior. After a while, he said, "Now it is your turn." He clicked on a slide and asked, "What do you see?" The photo was of a corpse lying on the ground. I zoomed in on what seemed to be the murder weapon—a rock as big as a hand that had a lot of blood on it. I said, "It looks like the murder was not premeditated or planned, because if the rock was the murder weapon, it was most likely a weapon of opportunity. You don't plan to murder someone with a rock." John looked at me, smiled, and said, "Good, you know your stuff." I didn't yet, but I went on to learn a lot from him, especially how to understand the true motives behind people's words and behaviors.

The third person is Johan Ahlberg, senior partner at McKinsey & Company, where I worked as a consultant. Johan gave me feedback on my development and performance. His typical message, which he delivered with clarity and appreciation almost every time we met, was "Stefan, you're doing well, but you are performing at about fifty to sixty percent of what you should be doing, and this is what you could do to improve. . . ." At the beginning, I thought that Johan was nuts, given that even before joining McKinsey I was, in comparison to most people I had met, constantly improving. But after a while I realized how cleansing and conducive to your development it is to be brave enough to focus on your shortcomings and how you can always do things better. Johan helped me up my game. He still does.

I would also like to thank two people who are close to me. One of them is my son, Ramses. In many ways, he is the inspiration for this book. He is a hard worker who follows his own convictions and path. His ability to always smile and have a positive outlook is admirable. Ramses is a true people person. He is helpful and supportive toward his friends, and I have never, ever, heard him say a negative thing about another human being—something I can't say about anybody else. That is inspirational, especially since he is only twenty-four and grew up at a time when negativity is the norm for most people.

The second is Regina, the love of my life, whose sheer number of abilities is inspirational. Her ability to stay true to a deeper purpose in life, cultivate good intentions and deeds personally and professionally, while constantly being one of the best at what she does—and in a sector of the business world where greedy men rule, and integrity is a word but not a practice—simply blows my mind. She is living proof of everything this book is about.

Finally, I want to thank the many people who contributed to the actual work with this book. Fifty-plus people read the manuscript (or parts of it) at early stages and gave me feedback that spurred its evolution. Through his coaching and editing, Josh Bernoff helped me come up with the original idea and structure for the book, including its proposal. Arthur Goldwag, with his sharp mind, unique ability to understand me and my thinking, and razor-sharp editing, helped make the final manuscript more crisp, clear, and logical.

But the person who had the most decisive impact on the final manuscript is Tim Bartlett, my editor at St. Martin's. He has step-by-step coached me to bring out things that needed to be in the book—things I did not think about since they are so ingrained in me by habit, but that were nonetheless critical to write about. Thanks to Tim's unceasing efforts, this is a more complete and helpful book. Thank you!

Introduction

Why I Wrote This Book

As a management consultant at McKinsey & Company, a leader of several multibillion-dollar corporate transformations, and a performance coach for business executives, military officers, and elite athletes all over the world, I have spent more than thirty years helping thousands of individuals, teams, and organizations to be intrinsically motivated—that is, to do what they do because they love the experience of doing it, and not because of the extrinsic rewards that come with it, such as money and status.

Helping people to love their work is gratifying, but observing the ripple effects is even more rewarding. Loving your work goes a long way toward helping you achieve goals you thought unattainable. My clients tell me that they have also become happier, healthier, and more fulfilled as a result of the work we've done together. I am here to tell you that I can do the same for you—provided that you are open to thinking in a different and better way about your work.

The first things my clients discover about me is that I don't tolerate bad thinking about work or life in general. I have no use for poor excuses, lies and deceit, ignorance, arrogance, selfishness, lack of focus on doing good by others, bad intentions, fear of the unknown, or taking the easy (lazy) way out when you should be biting the bullet. I come down painfully hard on any type of feeling-sorry-for-yourself sentiment, since that is just as handicapping as amputating your arms and legs. I call out these things in myself, too, not just in my clients. Not tolerating bad thinking helps me and my clients focus on what really matters. If a client persists in bad thinking, I simply cancel them.

Another bad habit I push my clients to avoid is shying away from pain. I experience as much emotional and psychological pain as anyone else, but unlike most people, I view them as necessary. First, emotional and psychological pain are signs that you are in a moment when your opportunity to grow is real and tangible. To try to avoid those moments, or to dream about a life without them, is to strive for a life of complete ignorance, without any true ambition. Second, you can't appreciate pleasure if you don't experience pain. The same is true for success and failure—you can't enjoy success if you don't experience failure. Unless you accept that emotional and psychological pain are both a part of life and a necessity for personal and professional growth, you won't get full value from the tools and principles in this book.

The idea to write this book came about after a keynote speech I delivered at a McKinsey & Company event. Having been a McKinsey consultant and for the past ten-plus years having coached countless junior and senior people at the firm, I had been asked to summarize my key insights. The theme of the speech was that immense pressure and constant challenges at work are blessings, since they force you to evolve. The secret to managing pressure is how you manage your mind. Many in the large audience were surprised, since they'd expected me to talk about how to *relieve* pressure, and then I said that pressure is good, provided that you know how to deal with it in a good way.

After my speech and the intense Q&A that followed, some

senior partners approached me and suggested I share my principles in a book. I had already written a booklet that had been circulating within McKinsey for some time. I knew that many McKinsey people I had not coached were using my ideas; the thought of reaching an even wider audience appealed to me. *Intrinsic Motivation* is the result.

It is my great hope that this book inspires you, but this is not a motivational book. I know already that I can't motivate you—the only one who can motivate you is *you*. What I *can* do is teach you how to master your mind so you can unlock the nearly unlimited potential you possess.

The tools and methods I will share with you are grounded in cutting-edge neuroscience and behavioral psychology. I have worked with and learned from some of the best-known people in those fields, including the late psychologist Mihaly Csikszentmihalyi, the psychoneuroimmunologist Nicholas Hall, and many others. My work even took me to the fantastic people at the FBI's Behavioral Science Unit (now called the Behavioral Analysis Unit, or BAU—you might be familiar with the fictional versions of it in the TV series *Criminal Minds* and the book and movie *The Silence of the Lambs*).

My experience as a corporate executive and coach, together with my work with these cutting-edge thinkers, taught me how to develop and hone essential principles and techniques that have proven highly effective. Apply them in an intentional and disciplined way, and you, too, will find yourself performing at a level well beyond what you would have thought possible.

That said, this is not so much a book for you to read and study as one for you to *use*. Follow my program, put the tools I will show you to work, carry out the daily practices I prescribe for rewiring your brain, and your life will change for the better.

Love What You Do

A lot of books promise big results. Why should you believe this one? For one thing, the techniques it prescribes have already been used by thousands of people at some of the biggest and most prominent companies in the world, and by high performers at that—people at the very top of their professions. Second, because I have lived out these principles myself since I was a lonely child in Örebro, Sweden, fifty years ago, when I stumbled on the five keys to my own and my clients' eventual success. They are:

- Never go to work (or school, or anywhere important) running on autopilot. For every task you undertake, have an explicit goal for an outcome and a set of tactics to achieve it.
- Never stop challenging and competing with yourself. You are the best measure of how much you have learned, improved, and grown.
- Consciously create emotional expectations for your experience of work and psych yourself up to meet or beat them. This is another way of saying that the attitude or mindset with which you approach your work is crucial.
- Review your work every day to make sure you make tangible progress that you can track and celebrate.
- Seek out and cultivate peers who share your excitement and positivity about work and from whom you can learn.

What all five keys have in common is the cultivation of *excitement*. Why is that so important? Because excitement enables you to *love what you do*. Loving what you do makes life worth living, but more important, it is *the* secret sauce for success and well-being!

When you love doing something, you'll want to do it a lot. And when you do something a lot, you get better and better at it, which further reinforces your enthusiasm. This leads to personal and professional development, because to keep loving the experience, you'll have to constantly increase its complexity and challenge. Musicians understand this—the reward of practicing boring scales is being able to perform more and more challenging compositions.

Furthermore, when you love doing something, you love thinking about it *before* you do it. This leads you to almost automatically have an exciting expectation for its outcome and a "plan" in mind for how to bring it about. You also love thinking about it afterward, which deepens your learning.

You may be saying to yourself, this is all well and good, but what if I hate my job? Here's the thing: *you can learn to love any activity.*

Don't Let Your Mind Invent Excuses for Not Loving Your Work

Before I began to write this book, I asked my son, Ramses, what he thought I should tell readers about myself. "Tell them that you're crazy," he said, "because that's what you are. You are the only person in the universe who does not know how to be bored. You're like a kid, excited about everything you do."

I agree with him about the second part—that I am excited about everything I do. But I'm neither crazy nor childlike.

How can I be excited about everything I do, even preparing my tax return? Because I have mastered my mind. Unfortunately, most professionals don't master their minds, which leads to a gazillion excuses about why they don't love their work.

The most common excuse I hear is the myth that they have too much to do, are too stressed, and need to reduce their workload. I have yet to meet a professional who has too much to do. The real reason they think they have too much to do is that they have not thought enough about how to execute smartly and efficiently. Most professionals can't describe how they go about executing their daily tasks, since they perform them on autopilot, without thinking about their approach or that it might include inefficient or outdated habits.

Other common excuses are poor relationships with colleagues, bad bosses, unfair performance assessments, and a lack of career opportunities. To be sure there are bad bosses, unfair or otherwise toxic work environments, and so forth. But, and it's a crucial but, most of those things are not why you hate your work, they are why you hate *where* you work. I am here to tell you that unless you are in an exceptionally bad working environment, in which case you should leave, your excuses are obstacles of your own creation.

When you don't love doing what you do, waking up and getting ready to go to work will be an effort. You will procrastinate, especially when it comes to tasks you think are especially difficult or dull or uncomfortable. You will finish your days exhausted, with little sense of pride or accomplishment.

When you don't love doing what you do, you will also become overly attached to extrinsic rewards, such as praise and money, since they are your compensation for your lack of enjoyment while doing the work itself. Failure becomes something painful, almost unbearable, given that you have put so much energy into something you don't even like.

When you are bored with your job or hate it, you get tunnel vision—you don't see the tasks you have to do in complete and holistic ways. This makes them even more boring!

But no matter what your excuses are for not loving your

work, they are not why you don't love it. The real reason is your own mind. Your mind creates these excuses because it is lazy, and it is lazy because you have failed to master it.

An unmastered mind is a lazy mind.

Making Work Lovable

Children come by their excitement naturally. Until it gets crushed out of them in school, kids innately know how to have fun and love what they do. Give them a wooden stick and watch as they begin to play with it. Wait a while and ask them what it is. You will get answers like "It's a car!" or "It's a rocket!" Kids have an unlimited capacity not just for fantasy and imagination (both powerful tools for self-improvement) but for engrossment, much as artists or athletes do when they are experiencing the mental state that my mentor Mihaly Csikszentmihalyi famously described as "flow." Simply put, flow is when your concentration is such that you lose all sense of time and place. The experience is its own reward; its end goal or outcome is just the icing on the cake. The satisfactions that go with creating an inspired work of art or flawlessly executing an athletic feat are easy enough to imagine. But as Csikszentmihalyi noted, "Most enjoyable activities are not natural; they demand an effort that initially one is reluctant to make." Some activities will only engross us if we take the trouble to pay close attention to them.

That is certainly true of work—it offers endless opportunities for engrossment. Why is that? Because it is so rich and complex. No matter what you do to make your living, it provides you with virtually unlimited opportunities to innovate and experiment, learn new things, seek new experiences, deepen your understanding of your relationships with the people around you, and learn how to solve a multitude of different problems.

So, why is it so hard for most professionals to love and enjoy all aspects of their work? Because unlike children, adults must work consciously and intentionally to cultivate their curiosity and their ability to be engrossed and to improve the ways they do things. That requires *deliberate thinking.* The challenge with deliberate thinking is that the key survival strategy we humans have evolved is to always secure a surplus of energy, which in many cases makes us lazy. Instead of thinking deliberately, we operate on habit, which allows us to save a lot of energy. How much energy does thinking take? Consider this: The average person running a marathon burns two thousand–plus calories. A chess player can burn as much as six thousand calories and lose up to two pounds per day during a tournament!

Given that thinking draws so much energy but is decisive for loving your work, this book offers you proven step-by-step tools and approaches that will make it *easier and less energy consuming for you to master your mind to think and act deliberately in your professional life.*

So please, stop wasting your time complaining or being bored by your work. Just think about how much of your time your work consumes. Not spending all of it in a way that excites you, that makes you evolve and grow and feel good about yourself, is tantamount to self-abuse.

Instead, use this book to turn your professional path into a nonstop adventure of growth, excitement, and goal fulfillment. I believe we owe it to ourselves to constantly seek ways to unlock our unlimited potential, and work gives us endless opportunities to do just that. Learn to love your work and you can reach any goal you set for yourself. As a human being, you are blessed with the most important tool you need to do this: your brain.

Use it!

The Habits and Attitudes of Professionals Who Love What They Do

People for whom work is its own reward share ten habits and attitudes. Ask yourself the following questions as you read about them: Does this describe my natural orientation toward my work? If your answer is no or not very much, then why is that? What is preventing you from embracing this habit or attitude? What benefits would you gain if you did?

1. **Boring is not in my vocabulary.** Intrinsically motivated people know there are no boring tasks, only boring ways to think about tasks. They identify what's exciting about every task they face.

2. **I meet every commitment.** Meeting your commitments creates a natural tension and focus in your work life. Every day becomes an opportunity to feel good about your capabilities and contributions.

3. **I learn from my mistakes and the awkward situations I find myself in.** You should be grateful for your failures (up to a point), because they focus you on what you need to work on.

4. **I have daily goals that are pragmatic, concrete, and focused on my development.** If you have an important meeting, visualize its best possible outcome. Then run a premortem in which you derive a concrete plan for opening the discussion, driving a certain perspective, interacting with an important attendee, and so on. Carry out a postmortem when the meeting is over, so you can find ways to improve your performance and develop new goals in the future. The feeling that you are progressing and growing is the biggest energy booster there is.

5. **I instantly assess what is strategically important and prioritize it.** Sort your development opportunities into three buckets: *always important, game changers,* and *not important now.* That last one is especially valuable because it allows you to take things off the table, reducing your stress and enhancing your ability to focus on what matters most.

6. **I use self-doubt as a goad for self-improvement.** Self-confidence is important, but taken to excess it can lead to complacency. Nothing is ever completely under control; a healthy amount of worry enables better performance.

7. **I seldom get distracted.** Distraction is a sign that you are focusing on things you can't influence. Focusing on what you *can* control—your own behavior—is a source of inner strength.

8. **I plan.** There are no truly complicated tasks, only complicated ways to think about them. Complicated thinking is the result of too little planning. Negative stress occurs when we haven't planned well enough.

9. **I view other people as assets.** The best way to learn how to do a new task is to copy from someone who does it well. You can also learn what to avoid by watching someone perform a task poorly.

10. **I seek coaching.** Not to motivate yourself or teach you how to develop—those are your personal responsibilities. A coach provides you with honest feedback on your performance. You don't have to like your coach, as long as you can trust the person to tell you what you need to hear.

How to Get the Most Out of This Book

Roughly half of the tools and principles in the book were developed when I was helping to lead turnaround efforts at a series of companies. Leaders and employees at all levels and in all roles adopted them, and they played a critical role in our success. Daniel H. Pink wrote about the work I did in his book *Drive: The Surprising Truth About What Motivates Us* (2009). All in all, the changes I helped put in place at those companies resulted in $2 billion in performance improvements.

The other half were developed during my work as an executive-performance coach, mostly during the ten-plus years I have spent working with project managers and partners at McKinsey & Company. McKinsey professionals combine a commitment to helping clients succeed with a focus on their own professional development. This made McKinsey the optimal laboratory for developing and testing these approaches.

The book is divided into three sections that reflect the progression most of my clients go through in our work together. It begins when they confront the biggest obstacle for their professional success and well-being: their own minds. Once they've applied the tools and principles I present in the first section, "Learn to Love Any Activity: Rewire Your Brain to Focus on Exciting Outcomes (FEO)," they are ready for the next: "Shape Your Destiny: Evolve Your Mindset to Become the Superstar You Can Be." Having addressed their own minds and mindsets, they are ready to apply the principles and tools I present in the third and last section: "Master the Second-Biggest Obstacle for Professional Success and Well-Being: Other People." The most foundational of these sections is the first. Until you learn to focus your tasks and activities on exciting outcomes (FEO), you will not love them.

To further guide you, I have sorted the tools into three levels, Easy, Moderately Demanding, and Demanding, depending on how difficult they are for typical professionals to implement in their work lives. What I mean by a "typical" professional is someone whose brain engages in work activities and tasks without any clear or exciting outcomes in mind, unless it's finishing the task or activity on time. If you operate like this, you will need to rewire your brain. That takes effort. Learning new things and breaking old habits requires a lot of brain energy.

The rule of thumb is that the more demanding the tool or principle you choose, the more effort you need to put in, but the faster you rewire your brain. The flip side is that you're likely to struggle or fail at first. Instead of continuing to use the tool until the full effect eventually emerges, some clients get frustrated and give up. That's where a lot of the value of my coaching comes in. I don't psychoanalyze my clients by exploring their childhoods and their dreams. I treat them more like a tennis coach would, teaching them the techniques they need to improve, then pressing them to practice them until these become second nature.

The less demanding tools require less energy and pain, but they work more slowly, and the slower you rewire your brain, the longer it takes to start loving what you do. This can also prompt you to give up.

No matter how easy or demanding the tool or principle you choose, your brain will protest. Inevitably, you will hear an inner voice telling you how badly your efforts are going and how huge the gap is between where you are and where you want to be. Since your brain wants to conserve its energy, it will provide you with any number of excuses to not pursue any change.

Patience and persistence are your allies. But two other things are equally important.

First, you need to force yourself to have fun when you experiment with the tools, even if you're simply planning your day. Bring your sense of humor! Laugh when you fail! What's true for kids is even more true for adults: *having fun feeds your appetite to learn.* It is the best medicine to cure your brain's pain and stop its relentless attempts to derail you with excuses.

Second, focus on the progress you have made after using one of these tools—every single time. To force you to quit, your brain presses you to focus on how short of your ultimate goals you are falling. That is the wrong metric. You should compare where you were before each attempt to use the tools, and where you are after. Each attempt to use one of the tools changes you. It builds your self-insight, and it builds your skills. No matter how little progress you make, there *is always* progress. That is what you should focus on!

To sum it all up: What is required from you is discipline, effort, and self-honesty. In addition, you should work to have fun and focus on the progress you have made using the tools. Once you get these things in place, you will be able to overcome your brain's initial resistance and develop your skills, change your behavior, and elevate your drive and performance. Nothing is "too difficult" or "impossible."

Let's Get Started

Regardless of who you are, what kind of work you do, or what you aspire to, these tools can serve you well. But they will work even better if you use them to achieve something that is important for you. If not, your efforts and enthusiasm are more likely to fade. That might cause you to feel bad about yourself or, worse yet, blame *me* for your failure. Blaming yourself is counterproductive and blaming me is like blaming Microsoft Word because you didn't write the book you always thought you had it in you to write.

The work turns on a six-step process:

1. Read the book and assess yourself—write down what you want to achieve.
2. Put your whole life in your calendar.
3. Minimize your turnaround time for simple tasks—perform them right away.
4. Commit to work daily to rewire your brain.
5. Create a simple routine for self-coaching—imagine me being there with you.
6. Create a support network—work this program with a buddy or with your team.

Read the Book and Assess Yourself

Think about things you *want* and *need* to achieve. It doesn't matter whether you have a specific goal or just want to enjoy your work more.

Ask yourself these questions: What do I struggle with? What keeps me up at night? What are my dreams and fantasies? Do I find it hard to fulfill my goals? Or to figure out which goal I should adopt? Am I actively evolving my mindset? Is the way I think about myself creating problems for me (or the people around me)? Do I want to improve my ability to understand and solve any type of problem? Do I need to improve the way I deal with people? Do I need to get my ideas accepted?

Whatever you want to achieve, write it down. Dare to be bold and aspirational.

Put Your Whole Life in Your Calendar

To work with my program, your calendar should hold a complete record of your life. Having a consolidated view of everything you have done and are supposed to do allows you to be time smart, in control, and to gamify your situation by competing with yourself. When you do things ahead of schedule, you will rightly feel a sense of achievement and control.

From now on, stop using checklists or other tools to track your life. Why? Because (1) checklists don't tell you how much time each item requires or when you are supposed to execute it; (2) things on a checklist get forgotten or lost; and (3) checklists don't give you a consolidated view of everything you are supposed to do, so they engender feelings of fragmentation and stress—you know you have a bunch of things to do, but you have no clear plan for when to pursue them.

Everything should go into your calendar view:

- Every work-related task and event you *know* you need to pursue, including your individual work tasks.
- Every work-related task and event you *think* you need to pursue, including your individual work tasks.
- Every work-related idea that you think you should pursue.
- Every private and personal task, event, and idea you know or think you need to pursue.

Whenever you come up with a task, event, or idea you know or think you should pursue, open your calendar immediately and select a time and a date for it. You can always change the date and time later; the purpose is not to hold you to a schedule, but to make sure that you have one. If a colleague calls you unplanned to discuss something and the discussion is interesting and gives you some insights, open your calendar, create a calendar event for when your colleague called, and use the insight as its title.

You can be certain that shit will happen at work. Why? Because you are dealing with people just like yourself, and none of us are perfect. A colleague might not treat you with the respect you think you deserve or decide not to do some-thing you mutually agreed should be done. Upper manage-ment might make a decision that confuses or upsets you.

When bad things happen, the challenge is to stay produc-tive and not get carried away by your emotions. This is hard for most of us. Sometimes it feels impossible to let go of the negative feelings. When that happens, you need to:

1. Open your calendar.
2. Select a time later that day to release your negative feel-ings.
3. Formulate the event in a solution-oriented manner; for example, "Think about how to deal with upper manage-ment's decision in a constructive way."

Now you can relax and get on with your work. Your un-conscious mind is working on the problem, and when it's time to deal with it consciously, you may actually come up with a solution. At the very least, you will be less likely to get carried away.

If you tend to blame others for your lack of progress or bad moods, this approach is also helpful. Simply open your calendar and select a time every week (or every day, if your brain is wired to feel vindictive a lot) as "Blame time." This way you don't have to dwell on how bad the people around you are; you have set aside a time for that. Eventually you will find that you have fewer and fewer things to whine about.

My Own Calendar-Use Case

I usually start my workday around 6:30 A.M. by checking my calendar in the week view. While I sip my coffee, I look over my past, present, and future tasks and events. My client sessions usually start around 8:00 or 9:00 A.M., so I ask myself, Are there any tasks that I have planned for later today, or tomorrow, or even later in the week that I could knock off right now? Usually there is at least one I can tackle right away. Given that my mind is fresh and I'm not tired, I can execute it effectively. This gives my sense of achievement and control a nice boost.

What do I do with the open space now left on my calendar? It depends. If I am feeling strong and energetic, I may revise the calendar to reflect what I've already accomplished. If not, I might leave the task at its original time. Why? Because when my smartphone pings me to remind me of the task and I have already done it, it will give me another boost. If I can't complete one of my assigned tasks in the time I allotted to it, I just push it forward. I have a number of tasks every week that for various reasons have to be rescheduled.

Minimize Your Turnaround Time for Simple Tasks— Perform Them Right Away

Don't be a hoarder of simple, brainless tasks as most professionals are. Be action oriented: always strive to perform simple, brainless tasks right away. Some examples:

- If you are in a meeting, and it is decided that another meeting is required—send out the meeting invitations for the additional meeting *right after* the meeting.
- If someone calls or emails you to request some information you have readily available, send it right away.
- If you are tasked with coming back with a simple suggestion or answer to a question, do it right away.

The rule of thumb is, if you have what is required and know how to perform the simple task, do it as soon as it arises! This helps you to (1) avoid a backlog of simple, brainless tasks, (2) shape the perception of yourself as a responsive and helpful professional, and (3) establish a sense of accomplishment.

If you can't perform simple, brainless tasks right away, then schedule them in your calendar.

Commit to Work Daily to Rewire Your Brain

The ultimate truth this book rests on is something I realized at an early age: *there are no boring or scary activities, only boring or scary ways to think about them.* How you think about an activity—before, during, and after—determines how you will experience it. This is a potentially life-changing insight.

Why is it so hard to derive enjoyment from what you do? Because you have not created the habit of thinking about what you do in a way that makes you intrinsically motivated. That is, you have not learned to focus on exciting outcomes (FEO), which I define as *always having an exciting outcome in mind for the tasks and activities you perform, as opposed to performing them on autopilot.*

The most powerful way to quickly rewire your brain to build that habit is via the Daily Goals method as described in chapter 10. Should you find that too demanding, then you should choose a less demanding method to start with, for example, (1) telling your family or friends about one thing that excited you at work every day (described in chapter 1), (2) selecting a daily theme (described in chapter 2), or (3) committing to daily journaling (described in chapter 7).

The critical thing is that you *commit to do this work every day.*

Create a Simple Routine for Self-Coaching—
and Imagine Me Being There with You

Routine is key to habit formation. Block out time on your calendar every Monday or Friday for a Weekly Planning Session (thirty to sixty minutes) and a Daily Learning and Reflection Session (fifteen to twenty minutes). Schedule your Daily Learning and Reflection Sessions toward the end of your workdays so you can note important takeaways. This will create a sense of achievement and closure and ensure that you maintain your FEO.

Imagine me being there with you during these sessions. As your coach, I would practice tough but deeply caring love:

- I'll ask you what is new and exciting in your life. If you can't answer, I'll ask you if you are an idiot. This is a little jarring for my clients at first, but they soon understand that I am serious and that this is essential to breaking their lazy mind habits.
- I don't let clients complain about their situations or give excuses for not having followed their routines. This approach is simple but nonnegotiable.
- I won't allow you to blame anyone else for any failure. Your focus must be on what you could have done differently to have avoided it. You can't control what others do.
- I'll ask you to tell me the three most important things you should focus on when performing daunting or uncomfortable tasks. When you switch from "This seems really difficult" to "What steps are necessary to get it done?," you will get it done!
- My clients and I laugh a lot—about the absurdities of everyday life, about how even the best approaches can be

upended by unforeseen events, and about the strange and wonderful people we meet in the world of work. Any developmental journey needs to be fun.

Create a Support Network— Work This Program with a Buddy or Within a Team

Once you begin your journey, you'll need to be careful about whom you engage with. Hanging out with the right people when you are trying to improve yourself is as important as eating the right foods when you are trying to lose weight.

Since I can't be there to support you as your coach (except in spirit), I strongly recommend that you work this book with other people. You can radically improve your chances of success by enlisting a buddy for mutual support, encouragement, and learning, as well for accountability. Meet for an hour weekly and reach out to each other for support whenever you need to. The weekly frequency is important to ensure progress and momentum.

You and your buddy should begin your sessions by sharing your achievements, challenges, and insights from the past week. Problem-solve around any challenges that you find particularly difficult, and share any insights you've had about yourselves, your priorities and challenges, and your contexts (e.g., your peers and staff, etc.). Then, look forward and share the key achievements you hope to accomplish in the coming week, as well as any challenges you anticipate. Problem-solve around the ones that you and your buddy believe will be particularly difficult. Then spend a few minutes jointly evaluating the coaching session: what worked well, what worked less well, and what you can improve next week.

It is critical that you and your buddy create a risk-free, confidential, and privileged zone—you are there to help each other, not compete. Talk about everything that needs to be talked about to secure progress, even if that means sensitive things such as your fears and traumas or anything else that holds you back. Grant each other 24-7 availability.

There should be only one rule: no excuses! Too many deviations from the program without legit reasons and the whole thing will fall apart.

In addition to working with a buddy, identify *role models* to learn from. Create a list of people who are good at what you want to achieve and ask them how they do it. Most will be delighted to share their insights.

Important: There are two types of people you should *avoid*: people who are negative and complain about their work, and people who might discourage you from pursuing your goals or even resent you for it. The first type produces nothing but garbage or pollution for your brain. The second are people who love the status quo and so will bad-mouth, confront, or outright bully people who threaten their "don't rock the boat" orientation. Make a list of the people around you that fit these descriptions and try to avoid them as much as possible. If you can't, then be very deliberate about how you deal with them.

If you are a team leader: Use the book with your staff! It is a great guide for creating concrete individual development plans as well as a tool for elevating people's performance and sense of well-being. Divide your staff into peer coaching teams, following the principles described above.

If you are the leader of a company or organization: Buy the book for your people and ask them to use the methods with their peers and leaders. If they start to use some of the tools and principles, you will see their productivity and job satisfaction improve.

In Conclusion . . .

The tools and approaches I present will make it *easy for you to rewire your brain to love any activity at work*. Do that and there's virtually no limit to what you can achieve. Whatever you do, don't let your brain derail you with excuses for not pursuing the success that is rightfully yours.

Learn to Love Any Activity

Rewire Your Brain to Focus on Exciting Outcomes (FEO)

The fastest and most effective way to learn to love any activity is to engage in *exciting outcome-focused behavior* (FEO) as opposed to *activity-focused behavior,* which is the norm among professionals.

I define FEO as always identifying exciting outcomes for the tasks and activities you perform and making concrete plans to achieve them. Let's be honest, most of us perform most tasks on autopilot, and that is a recipe for drudgery and eventually hating what you do. I put FEO at the heart of my coaching program because it has proven again and again, with clients of widely diverse backgrounds, to be the key to enjoying better mental health while increasing performance and skill development.

How common is FEO? Not common at all. Based on my expertise and experience, I believe the main reason professionals feel stressed, hate many of their tasks and activities, don't reach their goals, and perform far below their potential is because they are activity focused, not outcome focused.

To get your head around how to make FEO part of your normal way of operating at work, you need to understand that your work tasks have nothing to do with whether you love them. What makes a work task or activity lovable is how you think about the result you want it to achieve. The more exciting that result is to you, the more time you'll spend thinking about how to best perform that activity. The more you plan, the better you will perform. The better you perform, the more you will enjoy the activity. The more you enjoy the activity, the more you will want to do it. The more you do it, the better you will become at it. The better you become, the more you will need to increase its complexity to avoid boredom. The more you increase its complexity, the greater your sense of mastery. The greater your sense of mastery, the more power you'll feel to determine your destiny and the less vulnerable you'll be to changes in your workplace, the job market, and the professional world as a whole.

Why? Because mastery never goes out of fashion.

But if FEO is so simple to explain, why is it so challenging to apply?

There are many reasons, among them:

- **How we talk about work.** Work is often discussed as a necessary evil, not something you are supposed to love and enjoy.
- **How work achievements are rewarded in most organizations.** If professionals are activity focused, so are the organizations they work for. Organizations thrive on activity-based goals, such as "Develop the process for customer complaints," "Move our data to the cloud," "Implement agile as our way of working," "Become a customer-centric organization," or "Execute our digital transformation." The common denominator among almost all company goals is their lack of clear and exciting outcomes. Most professionals are evaluated and rewarded based on whether they have executed an activity and not on what they achieved by doing so.
- **A lack of skill.** If you have not practiced FEO, you will

lack the skill to define your wished-for outcomes. Building that skill takes practice.

- **Our biology.** We are wired to conserve energy. FEO requires you to think deliberately, which draws a lot of energy—at least initially, before you have turned it into a skill and a habit. But a flywheel effect occurs once it does become a habit.

Of all these challenges, that last is the most important for you to overcome, that is, your reluctance to expend energy on deliberate thinking. Once you do, you will:

Become detached from your outcomes but in love with your work to reach them. This may seem like a paradox at first, given your emphasis on focusing on exciting outcomes, but developing a healthy detachment from outcomes is a recipe for happiness, resilience, and success in work and life. Why? Because if you don't value the present, you won't love what you do.

What makes an activity exciting is your anticipation of it—all the thought and emotion you've invested in planning how you'll carry it out. The more thought and emotion you've invested in it, the more excitement you set yourself up to experience while you are executing it. In time, being engaged in the activity becomes even more rewarding than its expected outcome.

Rewiring your brain to master FEO will also allow you to **build a strong inner world that is capable of reframing the outer world.** If your inner world is strong enough, it can change the facts of your external world.

To show you how this works, I will share my own story. I spent most of my childhood playing by myself in my room, for two reasons. My dad's main role as a parent was to punish me, often with a spanking, whenever he thought I'd done something wrong—which in his mind was often. I was also overweight, which did not make me popular with other kids, who constantly bullied and ridiculed me. So, my room became my safe zone.

When you play alone, there is no one else to inspire you, to show you what to do, or how to enjoy it. Instead, you dialogue with yourself. The magical thing about the human brain is that if you force it to do something repeatedly, it becomes good at it. Playing alone for hours every day strengthened my imagination and ability to fantasize. Suddenly, I was not just a victim of the world around me. Since I could decide how to think about my world, I became more in charge of it.

Fantasize about becoming the most admired leader in your company, and it happens in your mind. When it does, your brain generates the same kinds of feelings that it would if you really were that person. But the most powerful thing about strong and repeated fantasies is that they create an urge to act them out. Why? Because just fantasizing will eventually not be enough. Instead, you will want to experience the real thing. I learned about the dark side of this tendency at the FBI's BAU, but it can also be a good thing.

This story very much applies to you when you work to master your FEO. At first, you will need to have daily dialogues with yourself about exciting outcomes. Over time, your brain will change and your inner world will grow. This will allow you to become more resilient in the outer world, with all its distractions and constraints—your bad boss, failed projects, or any other kind of bad experience. You will develop the capacity to reframe how you think about them in much more constructive ways.

When you master FEO, you will also improve your ability to manage stress. Defining an exciting outcome for an activity has the same positive effect as making a decision, in that it gives you a sense of direction and control.

When you lack a sense of direction and control, it's harder to be in the present moment. This makes us anxious, since the Default Mode Network (DMN) in our brain gets too much bandwidth. Typically, you spend about 30 percent of your waking time in the DMN; it hosts your abilities to fantasize, daydream, and reflect on the past and future, including your social life and relationships. But too much thinking about that makes us ruminate and feel anxious. (*Was the past really that good? Does the future really look that great?*)

Furthermore, defining an exciting outcome is a powerful way to defuse anxiety in uncomfortable situations. We all get anxious sometimes. When we do, we don't want to think about what's causing it, because just thinking about it is painful. This makes us less prepared for whatever it is and hence even more stressed. Defining an exciting outcome for the situation can help you disassociate yourself from it emotionally.

Engaging in FEO every day will radically increase your ability to see what is important in any situation, task, or activity and **strengthen your ability to prioritize.** No matter how much is coming at you, you'll be able to decide what really requires your time and why and how best to deal with it. This is because you will develop deeper insights into yourself, better professional skills, and a greater understanding of the context in which you operate.

The reason for these benefits is simple: FEO strengthens your ability to think in terms of results. When this becomes your default thought pattern, you will be much more flexible in how you perform your tasks as well as in how you prioritize the subtasks within them when you are under pressure.

And finally, mastering FEO will **strengthen your indirect**

reward system. Human beings have two reward systems, one direct and one indirect. The *direct reward system* is strong, operates quickly, and is hard for us to control. Its focus is on instant gratification, which makes us susceptible to bad habits such as gambling, eating too much sugar, giving up on working toward goals, and shying away from challenges. Our *indirect reward system* is much slower, weaker, and less developed, so we need to work to strengthen it. Working to master FEO every day pushes you to think explicitly about what we hope to gain from a task and what we need to do to get it. Elite athletes probably have the most well-developed indirect reward systems of anyone; otherwise, they would not be able to persist through all the challenges and pains that being an elite athlete entails.

How to Master FEO

You need to accept two things before you set out to master exciting outcome-focused behavior.

First, that your work activities or tasks *have no inherent traits*. The task does not tell you, "Hi there, my name is Departmental Meeting, and I am very boring." It is 100 percent within your power to think about your activities in ways that make them lovable. One embarrassingly simple way to make an activity lovable is to focus on its importance to the people who depend on the results you create. I will tell you what I tell my clients: If you think an activity is boring, then *you* are the one who is boring. Don't blame your tasks. They are innocent.

Second, *all* of your work activities possess unlimited complexity, which means they could and should be performed with endless variation. Proactively embracing the complexity and richness of your tasks is a bulletproof way for you to become immersed or engrossed in them, just as the child you once were became engrossed in building a sandcastle.

Accept the need to work to master the complexity of your tasks and a wonderful new world opens up to you, one with unlimited opportunities to improve. You will always be able to figure out new ways to perform a task faster, increase its output, and/or improve the quality of its result.

The opportunity to improve collaborative tasks is especially gratifying. In my experience, professionals have unlimited ways of wasting one another's time—everything from ignoring or interrupting one another to being poorly prepared for meetings or presentations. As simple a task as asking a colleague for information can be performed in a much more rewarding and valuable way. To do that you should reflect on:

- What exactly do I need to know and how do I express it?
- Why is it important for me to know this and is this the right time?
- Is my colleague the right person to ask or are there others who are more suitable?
- Is there anything I need to know that is available in ways other than talking to this colleague?
- If talking to this colleague is the best and most efficient way to find out what I need to know, how do I organize the conversation so that I minimize use of my colleague's time?
- Is there anything I can do that will make my colleague feel that he or she has gained something from the conversation?

Every task, no matter how seemingly monotonous, can be made interesting, and believe me when I tell you that people will begin to notice that their interactions with you are refreshingly frictionless and often yield unexpected value. They will treat you differently. And you will begin to feel better about yourself and work.

The Five Cognitive Elements That Drive FEO

In my own effort to maximize my clients' time, I have sought to clarify the key elements that drive FEO. In truth, though, they are all things I discovered nearly fifty years ago, and they work as well for my clients today as they did for me when I was a child.

When I was eight, my mom rented a piano, and I fell in love with it instantly. Much to my mom's annoyance at first, when I was still learning, I spent hours practicing. An important step in my development occurred when I began to compose my own songs and play them for my classmates during our weekly music hours at school. By the time I was ten, I was invited to play at graduation and other school events. Life was great: I was doing what I loved, and other people seemed to like what I was doing.

Well, maybe life was not so great; once music took over my life, my grades began to slip. By the time I was fourteen, I was told my poor grades would put a ceiling on my college prospects. This made me anxious, and the anxiety prompted me to see myself and my situation in a new light. I was no doubt a damn good musician, but I was mediocre at everything else.

Thinking about the future, I realized I needed to improve at school and quickly, because given the fierce competition, the probability of my having a successful career as a musician was low. But how could I improve? Studying was so dull compared with what I experienced playing music.

So, I asked myself the question that has made a world of difference ever since: What if I could identify what makes playing music so enjoyable and apply that to studying? I thought about what made playing the piano so enjoyable. Gradually, I realized that there were five things:

1. **I was passionate about creating a beautiful end product.** Whether I was practicing on my own or playing for an audience, I always fantasized about the end product. Before I sat down to play, I imagined what I was going to play and how it would sound. If I was going to play for an audience, I would fantasize about the expressions I wanted to see on people's faces as I played.

2. **I was constantly challenging and competing with myself.** I was always mindful of the skills I needed and wanted to improve. *I had a plan and set goals* when I practiced that were demanding but concrete, such as playing a song at an almost impossibly fast tempo but with perfect precision, or playing the same song ten times without making a single mistake. I was surgical in my analysis when I did not deliver on the challenges I had set myself: *Why am I not able to do this? What do I need to do differently?* This thinking process was engrossing and exciting, and it made me feel in charge and in control.

3. **I cultivated deliberate expectations of the emotional experience I wanted while playing.** When I wasn't playing the piano, I imagined how I would feel when I was. If I felt mellow as I was coming home from school, I imagined myself playing a ballad to either manifest or celebrate my mood. If I was in a bad mood, I would think about what I could play that would cheer me up and give me positive energy.

4. **I could always monitor my progress.** Given the first three

keys I have just described, I could track my progress daily. That not only secured but elevated my intrinsic motivation; knowing you are progressing and becoming better at what you do is a rush and is highly addictive. I wanted to relive that feeling over and over. Every time I finished playing the piano, I started looking forward to my next session.

5. **I viewed fellow musicians as a source of inspiration.** One thing that made playing the piano so enjoyable to me was being able to talk with other musicians about it. The exchange of ideas, experiences, and advice fueled our ambition and motivation.

Applying the Five Cognitive Keys to My Studies and My Professional Life

Once I discovered these keys, I began to apply them to studying. I would challenge myself by intensely focusing on what I had a hard time understanding, including why I found it so difficult. Before each study session, I would envision the emotional experience I wanted and, based on that, plan how I would pursue the session, even down to where it would take place—my bedroom, the library, outdoors.

I approached my classwork in a similar way, with clear up-front thinking about what my desired end product and emotional experience were, both during and after class.

I also started to view my classmates differently. I observed who seemed to be most interested in math, who were the most interested in natural sciences, and so on. Then I would proactively engage them in conversation, and they became sources of insight and inspiration.

The result? Almost immediately, I began to enjoy my schoolwork much more. Within two years, my grades had improved so much that my options for higher education became almost unlimited. I felt proud the day I graduated.

These five cognitive elements determined my approach to my studies at university, and they have been decisive for how I have approached my professional life and life in general. They helped me get my head around becoming first a copywriter, and then an art director. They helped me to grow and get hired as a creative director at a fashion magazine. They were completely decisive for my transformation into a management consultant at McKinsey & Company. They certainly helped me to become productive in a variety of executive roles, from head of operational development to chief financial officer. They serve me and my clients well in my work as an executive coach.

They will serve you, too.

So let's get started. In the pages that follow, I will describe proven tools and principles that will allow you to master exciting outcome-focused behavior. I have sorted them in the order of how easy or demanding they are to implement. Be aspirational but realistic in which you choose to start with.

1

Set Expectations Every Day, and Bring Home Something Exciting and Interesting to Tell Your Kids

Easy to implement in your work life

One easy way to start rewiring your brain is to actively manage your expectations for your workday. Easier still is simply expecting to experience something exciting—priming yourself in this way will make you aware of it when it happens.

As mentioned above, most of us simply wake up and go to work without a thought about our expectations or goals for the day. Is this a problem? Yes, because you get the experiences you deserve. If you have no expectations for your workday, chances are you will experience nothing more than a typical dull day. If you expect negative things, chances are you will experience those. The same goes if you expect positive things.

One of the smartest things I ever read was contained in the welcome note to parents from the principal of my son's school when he entered the first grade: "Make sure you tell your kids about something positive you experienced during your day. It is important that kids have positive expectations for how it is to be a grown-up."

I took it to heart. Every day on my way home from work I thought about what I would share with my son. Soon I noticed that I was also thinking ahead, about the experiences I hoped to share with him at the end of the day tomorrow, and the day after that. In the beginning I focused primarily on positive experiences, for example, the nice feedback I got from colleagues, or tasks I had performed better than I'd expected. But over time, I also began to share some interesting challenges I was facing, and even some failures. I was careful never to blame others for them, and to include my thoughts about how I could do things better.

So here's the simple task that I give every single one of my clients: At the end of the workday or on your way home, write down the thing(s) that you felt were exciting and share them over dinner. Then, when you brush your teeth before bed, think about what could potentially be exciting tomorrow. Review it once again before you go to work in the morning. I found this to be an almost effortless way to ensure that every day at work was special.

2

Pursue a Daily Theme That Excites You

Easy to implement in your work life

You'll find immediate payoff from your efforts to begin and end each day with a focus on how to make work exciting. Congrats, you've already begun to rewire your brain for FEO, not to mention set a good example for your family. You can continue the rewiring by setting a single theme for each workday, for example, "Today I am going to learn something new about my colleagues" or "Today I will focus only on the positive side of things."

Write down your theme. (You'll notice that I ask you a lot to write things down. I strongly suggest you keep a simple notebook on you for this purpose.) Also, think about moments when you might be tempted to diverge from the theme (say, a regular meeting you find particularly tiresome, or an interaction with a difficult colleague). If you are able to identify these situations in advance, you'll increase your chances of being able to redirect your thoughts toward the positive.

You can also write down negative thoughts as they occur, including at what times and the contexts. Then compile the thoughts in a brief summary before you go home, listing how many and what kind, why, and in what contexts. Just making this simple compilation will be rewarding since (1) you will get a fact-based view on how many negative thoughts you had, when, and why; (2) it will help you get them out of your system so you can relax; and (3) you will activate your unconscious mind to problem-solve on how you can better deal with situations that provoke negative thinking. Run with that theme for a week or longer and you will not only learn a great deal about yourself and what causes your negative thoughts, but will also actively rewire your brain to think more positively.

3

Use If-Then "Implementation Intentions"

Easy to implement in your work life

One scientifically proven way to drive FEO is to explicitly define and write down a set of "implementation intentions"—a concept that Peter Gollwitzer, professor of psychology at New York University, introduced in 1999.[1] An implementation intention can be formulated as "If/when X happens, then I will do Y" or "If/when X happens, I will do Y and avoid doing Z."

Here are some examples from my clients:

- "If team members or colleagues make a mistake in their work, I will take a deep breath, show a friendly face, and say, 'Let's see what we can learn from this.'" (Charles, director of an R&D team)
- "To improve my people-development skills, I will set aside fifteen minutes every day to write down one thing that each team member or colleague did well, and one thing that each team member or colleague can improve." (Wendy, leader of a marketing team)
- "If I am forced to perform complicated tasks when it is late and I am tired, I will spend ten minutes thinking about what I need to pay special attention to in order to avoid making mistakes." (Peter, senior analyst at a hedge fund)

This works especially well if your implementation intentions are linked to specific times during the day, such as, "At seven P.M. every workday, I will drop what I am doing and spend fifteen minutes doing my daily journaling." Put it in your calendar!

By identifying the situations and your actions beforehand, you create a platform on which to automate your goal-oriented actions over time. This works better than being forced to figure out what you should do in the moment, which takes a lot of energy and willpower and so can lead you to revert to your undesired behaviors.

So, at the end of each workday, write down what worked well and less well in your implementation intentions. Act the next day on the things that did not work well.

4

Master the Art of Baby Steps

Easy to implement in your work life

When the human mind is described in books and articles, it is often portrayed as a beautiful and magnificent "tool" or "machine." I agree up to a point, but I sometimes find it more on point to describe it as being more like a brilliant but *very* stubborn child.

Even though I am an expert on personal productivity, possess a reasonable level of self-knowledge, and know a lot about the human mind, my own mind often refuses to cooperate with me. This is particularly the case when it identifies a task or situation as daunting, which it does whenever the stakes are high and there are difficulties.

Whenever I think about such a task or situation, my mind runs through all the ways I could fail. It is extremely painful for my poor head to host all those negative thoughts, and no matter how hard I try, I simply can't get rid of them. As a result, I am virtually paralyzed. This is much worse than mere procrastination; it is sheer terror. My mind convinces me that I can't succeed, no matter how hard I try. One of the many situations in my life when this happened was when I was finalizing the manuscript for this book.

After I signed the contract with my publisher, I had seven

weeks to complete and deliver a final manuscript. I had already written about 85 percent of the book. I just had to write five or six new chapters and make some small tweaks and additions to the ones I'd already written. Objectively, the assignment was perfectly doable.

My first goal was to come up with a plan. But when I sat down to do so, I was filled with doubt. Knowing myself, or rather my own mind, I simply gave up. I remember thinking, "Tomorrow is another day and I am sure my mind will cooperate then." But a negative spiral began. The result was a lack of sleep and little progress. After a few days of that, I said to myself, "Enough is enough."

The first thing I did was try to write down why my mind viewed finalizing the manuscript as so impossible. I came up with:

- I didn't want to let my editor and the team at the publisher down.
- I didn't want to let myself down after all the effort I had put into writing the book.
- I didn't want to let my clients down by not being as available to them as I usually am during that seven-week period.
- It had been four months since I last worked on the book, and getting back into the right frame of mind for book writing would take time and dedicated effort.

Just clarifying this for myself was helpful. But if it was a step in the right direction, it was still not enough. Now I had to decide what my approach should be. I realized I had to view finalizing the manuscript as a completely new and unfamiliar task. I had to take *baby steps,* an approach that is based on the following principles:

1. **Start anywhere but start early!** Forget about logic and what is the right thing to start with—just start anywhere. In my case, I decided to start with the first thing that came to mind, the introduction—no matter how significant or insignificant it was in the big scheme of finalizing the manuscript. But it could have been anything—the key was to get moving. You have to start early. It is crucial. The worst thing you can do is wait; the closer you get to the deadline, the more paralyzing the anxiety you will experience and the less able you will be to think clearly and be productive. In my case, I had lost one week but had six weeks left, which was still a lot of time given that the amount of work was not that great.

2. **Celebrate the time spent, not the result!** Though I normally emphasize the importance of defining exciting outcomes, when your mind is stubbornly fixated on the impossible, it's important that you not set demanding targets or focus too much on the result you must achieve. Why? Because no matter what result you generate, your mind will shoot it down and try to convince you that it sucks. Instead, just focus on the time you should spend. In my case, I decided to spend ten minutes on the introduction and just write down what came to mind. I did not care if the results were brilliant. I just celebrated that I had spent ten minutes working. I continued that approach for a week.

3. **Gradually increase the time you spend and focus on results.** A good idea when you schedule your baby steps is to make sure you have free time after. Why? Well, chances are that you will suddenly find yourself immersed in what you are doing. If so, you should stay immersed, since that will most likely lead to good results. I scheduled my ten or fifteen minutes of baby steps in blocks when I knew I

could spend as much as another hour or two. Once your mind agrees that you have made tangible progress, it is ready to not only accept but also define your exciting outcomes in a helpful and progressive way.

This approach works for me and my clients every time; you just need to know when to use it.

5

Learn like the Terminator

Easy to implement in your work life

The ability to effectively draw relevant insights, learn what is important, and build expertise plays a big role in differentiating merely good employees from those who are essential. If you've seen the movie *The Terminator*, starring Arnold Schwarzenegger as a cyborg, you know that the Terminator constantly scans his environment to assess threats and opportunities, while absorbing new information necessary to carrying out his mission. He provides an excellent example of effective and almost effortless learning.

How is this relevant for you? Well, you have the same capability for effortless learning that the Terminator has. Unfortunately, the tendency to stumble through life without purpose means this capability remains untapped and unmanaged in most professionals, which leads to problems as well as a lack of personal and professional growth.

Leverage Your Mind's Bad Boy: The Confirmation Bias

Perhaps the most damaging unmanaged capability we have is confirmation bias, the mother of all cognitive biases. The American Psychological Association defines it as "the tendency to gather evidence that confirms preexisting expectations, typically by emphasizing or pursuing supporting evidence while dismissing or failing to seek contradictory evidence."[1]

Most descriptions of confirmation bias focus on its negative effects. For example, if we only see what we want to see, we won't learn anything new. If I have a negative view of a person, chances are I will only see things that support that view when I engage with the person, missing out on potentially positive sides. If I think I have a brilliant idea for what to do, I will only see the data and insights that support it. Consequently, most of what you hear about confirmation bias is that it needs to be "overcome."

I counsel my clients to think differently about confirmation bias. First, there is no way to overcome or turn off your confirmation bias. Confirmation bias is a force of nature. Our minds automatically form expectations and beliefs about what we are supposed to look for because they cannot operate properly under uncertainty. Hence, the problem with confirmation bias isn't that it exists, but that we *don't take a step back from it and consciously configure it to serve us.* For you, this means configuring your confirmation bias to support true learning in the moment.

To give you an idea of how this works, I want to tell you about a master listener. In the late 1990s, when I was about six months into my tenure at McKinsey & Company, a senior partner invited me to join him at a client meeting to discuss the progress of a complex project involving several hundred people. The clients gave us a lot of input about what they thought was working and what they wanted to work better. I took notes like crazy, while the senior partner listened, asked questions, and made suggestions. When the meeting was over, my head hurt with all that I had taken in.

When we got in the car, I asked the senior partner how I

should debrief the other team members. "Just give me a minute," he said, picking up his phone. "I want to leave a voice mail for the team." Back then, we used group voice mail for updates and insights (leaving voice mails is an immensely more powerful way to draw insights and learning than writing emails, as we tend to think things through more clearly and choose our words more carefully when we prepare oral presentations). "Hi, team," he said into his phone. "Stefan and I have just finished a meeting with the client team, and I want to share the key insights and implications with you so we all have time to prepare for tomorrow's team meeting." He then gave a sixty-second distillation of the discussion, highlighting what was working and why, as well as the areas where less progress was being made and the reasons for that. I could not believe how effortlessly and correctly he summarized the discussion. But that was not all. He then gave each team member two or three assignments to prepare for the next day's team meeting.

I was flabbergasted. How was it possible to boil a four-hour meeting down to its essence and prepare an agenda for a new meeting in just a few minutes? Was he human or a robot?

The answer is simple: he had reconfigured his confirmation bias to support true learning in the moment. His bias was not oriented toward confirming what he wanted to be true; he had reoriented it toward *confirming what the team would need to do next*.

This technique starts with the question "What am I supposed to do with the information and learning that I get in this meeting?" Information and learning that you cannot use practically tends not to stick or register. The senior partner knew that he needed (1) to give an accurate account of the overall progress of the project, and (2) to guide each team member to a set of priorities that would bring the lagging areas of the project up to speed. To this end, he structured his confirmation bias to home in on the answers to these questions:

- What is the overall progress of the project? Which areas are progressing well and why? Which areas are progressing less well and why?
- Which team member is responsible for each area that is progressing less well?
- What should each responsible team member do from now until tomorrow's team meeting to develop a plan to get the problem areas up to speed?

The senior partner used this structure both to sort the information and learning he collected and as a basis for an action plan. It allowed him to stay focused, zooming in on what was important and discarding what was irrelevant or less important.

You can use this technique, too. First, you need to define your desired learning outcome. Then, you create a structure for your learning and use it to both target your questions and test your ideas during the meeting, while sorting and organizing your most important insights. Immediately after the meeting, you should do a *recall*—a quick summary—without referring to your notes or any written materials.

All professionals must develop deliberate ways of learning and studying, similar to the techniques they used when they went to school.

The larger point is that you should think about how you take in, process, and use information and look for ways to improve.

Some time ago I took a wonderful online course called Learning How to Learn by Barbara Oakley, a professor at Oakland University in Michigan.[2] I strongly recommend you take it yourself, but in the meantime, here are some of the techniques I learned.

If you are reading an important article, paper, or chapter in a book relevant for your work, start by (1) skimming the material and writing down what you see as its two or three key themes. Then, (2) read it carefully and under each of the key themes write (a) what you already know, (b) what was new, and (c) what you perhaps did not understand. (3) Put the material and your notes away. Take a blank sheet of paper and do a recall—try to remember the themes and what you wrote under them. Recall is a powerful way to ensure you retain material—much more so than if you read it again. Then, (4) compare your original notes with your recall exercise. Focus on what you still don't understand and create concrete strategies for getting your head around it, either by looking for more to read or by identifying an expert to talk to.

Other tips and tricks for learning:

- Whenever you are struggling with an idea or problem, think about how you could explain it to a child.
- Don't just think about your explanation, say it out loud or write it down. The additional effort of speaking and writing helps convert it into neural memory structures.
- Write by hand. Handwriting builds stronger neural structures in memory than typing.
- Space your repetitions when learning something new, just as athletes do with physical exercises. Your brain is like a muscle, it can handle only a limited amount of exercise on one subject at a time.
- Test and quiz yourself randomly on different types of problems you are trying to understand better or solve.

6

Create a Time Budget and Track Your Time Every Day

Easy to implement in your work life

Professionals who love what they do have a loving relationship with time. That is because they know that time is our most precious asset, and thus they invest it wisely. They want to maintain a healthy balance between work, hobbies, family, and friends and realize the key to this is to stop wasting time.

I think we've finally reached the point where most of us realize that long working hours are not evidence of high performance, but rather some combination of laziness, disorganization, and a lack of preparation and planning. I emphasize this the first time I meet my clients, and at every meeting after.

Most of my clients come in with a difficult relationship with time; they often tell me they feel oppressed, that they have too much to do and too little time to do it. I begin by asking them what they could do to help the situation, and their typical answer is "I either need to give up some of my tasks, or I need more resources." Interestingly, when I ask them how they perform their tasks, most can't tell me. That's because they perform them out of habit, almost without thinking. Not surprisingly, they seldom consider whether there are smarter and more effective ways to approach them.

I guarantee my clients that if they adopt a few proven tactics and habits regarding time, they will soon have all the time they need and more. I will make that same guarantee to you.

Time Habit 1: Spend Less Time on the Task While Maintaining or Improving Your Performance

The logic is simple: to work less but maintain or increase your performance, you must do things differently and, perhaps, do different things. Six steps lead to this time habit.

Step 1: Analyze your starting point. How much do you really work? Include the time you spend thinking about work when you're off the clock, since that can create the feeling "I am always working," that is, when you are spending precious time with your family. You need to know how to relax and clear your mind. Related to this is the recurring phenomenon known as the Sunday blues, the stress and anxiety people experience when they anticipate all the things that will happen at work during the next week.

Step 2: Define the burning platform. This is another form of focusing on creating an exciting outcome. Think about how you'd use the hours you'd save. Write it down.

Step 3: Prepare your time budget. Define the total number of hours you want to spend on work each week, including the time you spend thinking about work, and the time you want to spend on other things, such as your hobbies and your spouse, family, and friends. The word *budget* is decisive, since it connotes that time is intrinsically precious, something you need to handle every bit as carefully as you do your money. What you do and, more important, what you achieve will determine whether the time you spent was a good investment. If it was not a good investment, what should you have done differently?

Step 4: Make it difficult for yourself—do a step further. If you believe that a good time budget for work is cutting back to forty-five hours per week, then push yourself more and commit to getting to thirty-five hours. Even though that might be virtually impossible to achieve, striving to achieve it will accelerate your skills, performance, and development.

Step 5: Define your ideal workweek on a spreadsheet. Distribute your weekly time budget per workday on a spreadsheet. For example, Mondays you will start working at 8:30 A.M. and finish at 5:00 P.M.; Tuesday you will start at 8:00 A.M. and finish at 6:00 P.M.; and so on.

Time Tracking				
Monday				
Planned start time	Actual start time	Planned end time	Actual end time	Insights and learnings

Step 6: Track your start and end time every day. Track your start and end times on your prepared spreadsheet and reflect upon the following questions:
- Did I deliver on my time budget?
- If not, why?
- What insights do I want to leverage going forward?

Time Habit 2: Stick to Your Guns

Here is a common trap you need to avoid. Let's say you typically finish at 8:00 P.M., plan to finish at 5:00, but actually finish at 6:30. Because this is an improvement, you might be tempted to relax. The problem with thinking this way is that it is a slippery slope. Soon you will be back where you started. So, particularly at the outset, do *everything you can* to finish on time—you need to be meticulous and make a concerted effort to deliver on your commitment.

Time Habit 3: Treat Every Deviation as an Opportunity to Improve

Naturally, there will be days when you cannot deliver on your plan. On these days, it's crucial to zero in on what caused you to miss your goal and analyze what it will take to eliminate it.

Time Habit 4: Be Clear About Your Available Time for Team Projects and Tasks

If you work on more than one collaborative project, it's important to be up-front with the people you are working with about how much time you can spare. Many of my clients who manage multiple tasks experience constant stress over not spending enough time on each one.

Once you are clear about how much time you can spend, then work with your colleagues to make the most of it. Develop an operating model with them and review it weekly. This increases your sense of control and ownership over your time, and enables you and your collaborators to become even smarter about how to best leverage it.

7

Commit to Daily Journaling

Easy to implement in your work life

We do not learn from experience. We learn from reflecting on experience.

—JOHN DEWEY

Life can only be understood backwards; but it must be lived forwards.

—SØREN KIERKEGAARD

Daily journaling offers a powerful way to FEO. Spending fifteen to twenty minutes every day on writing, reflecting, and learning is a simple way to create a greater sense of control and achievement, which reduces stress and anxiety. Writing surfaces your performance weaknesses, allowing you to become more fact based and granular in your self-understanding, and enabling greater precision in how you drive your development.

Journaling is fundamentally about reflecting on your experiences. Scientific research confirms the benefits of daily reflection and learning; tests show that people who reflected upon how they accomplished a task or solved a problem performed much better than those who didn't when both groups undertook a similar task or problem again.[1]

You might ask, Why reflect in writing? Is it not enough to simply sit down and think through your day? The answer, as already mentioned, is that writing creates much stronger neural structures than mere thoughts. Our working memory is limited; we have a much harder time drawing complete insights from fleeting thoughts than we do a written product. Writing is also effective in regulating our emotions; when we are upset or excited, journaling brings us back down to earth. And finally, writing requires us to organize and edit our ideas, sharpening our thinking skills.

Most of my clients use daily time tracking and journaling together, with powerful results. Most experience a deeper sense of control and a much deeper level of learning about themselves and their contexts. A few have been able to reduce their work time by 15 or 20 percent while accelerating their development and performance.

Here are two important tips for successful journaling: First, block out a recurring time on your daily calendar for it so you don't forget to do it. Commit to doing it, even on days when you are under stress or time pressure. You will find it a powerful release on such days, as well as a way to regain control and agency.

Last year I witnessed a powerful example of the benefits of daily journaling. A client, a senior executive at a global corporation, was promoted to sales director of his company's biggest and most successful region. We'd started to work together a few months before he took on his new role, creating a detailed plan for his first hundred days.

For the first six weeks after my client moved to the region and took on his role, we met biweekly via Zoom. I felt that perhaps things were not going that well, which was confirmed when I flew overseas to spend a few days with him. While I was there, I gathered 360-degree feedback on his progress from his stakeholders.

The feedback was ice-cold. He spent most of his time in his office, I was told. He hardly participated in meetings, and when he did say something, he did not contribute or lead. Furthermore, his direct reports found him inaccessible. When I shared this with him, he admitted that he was overwhelmed. First, "everything" already worked well in the region, so what could he possibly contribute? Second, the territory was too big and complex for him to get his head around. And third, he felt immense pressure not to let down his previous boss—the one who had promoted him. I felt overwhelmed myself just listening to him!

I told him there were no silver bullets: he would have to work himself into his role. We agreed that daily reflection and journaling offered a structured approach to figuring out the dynamics in his new work environment—for example, his colleagues' and direct reports' ways of working—and that it would help to make his progress or lack of progress more tangible. Our plan going forward was for him to share his daily journaling with me. We would have weekly check-ins via Zoom in which we would talk through what he'd done that week and what he was expecting to do in the week coming up. Though I am typically optimistic, I was concerned, given the issues he faced, not to mention his being halfway around the world, fourteen time zones away from his former peers and friends.

After a month, I began to notice a change. There was a sharpness to his reflections, to the story he told about what was going on around him, about the behavior and performance of his team, and of what needed to improve. I sensed he was feeling more in control. His description of his own performance suggested that he felt he was improving. But I was not with him, so I did not know for sure. After four months, I did another 360-degree feedback, including all his direct reports.

I talked to twelve people, and the experience stunned me. Everyone I talked to told me my client had become a different person—that after a shaky start, he was fully on top of his role. He proactively participated, led, contributed, and was accessible to all his stakeholders. Of course, he had made this happen by changing his approach, not merely by committing to journaling. But the journaling had helped him acknowledge his challenges and commit to overcoming them.

Cathy provides another extraordinary example of the power and benefits of daily journaling. Today she is a high performer who enjoys every aspect of her work, but when I met her, she was a junior consultant at McKinsey & Company who had just received a devastating performance review. Here is her story, in her own words:

> *Grant me the serenity to accept the things I cannot change, courage to change the things I can, and wisdom to know the difference.*
>
> The Serenity Prayer immediately comes to my mind when I think about the benefits I have experienced from daily journaling. It's helped me to gain self-insight, create a sense of control and power, take responsibility over my destiny, accept "what is" instead of wishing that things were different, and, most important, move into action.
>
> When daily journaling was introduced to me, I was at rock bottom. I had joined McKinsey a year before, but things did not go as I planned. Early on I started to feel isolated, mostly because it took a long time to find a relevant client project to work on. When I finally got one, I immediately sensed that I was not good enough compared to my peers and colleagues. It was a self-fulfilling prophecy and a vicious circle. I felt helpless. I could not think straight and I was virtually clueless about what to do.

Then daily journaling was introduced to me. Almost immediately, things started to change for the better: it helped me with both emotional healing and professional growth. Writing about my experiences enabled me to distance myself emotionally from them, see them from different angles, think constructively about what I could learn from them, as well as what I should do differently next time.

By simply reflecting on my interactions with others, my key achievements, and my emotional state—and thinking about why certain dialogues played out as they did, or why my emotional state was as it was—I got deeper and deeper into myself. Soon I discovered that my previous personal experiences were a big part of why I was struggling. That gave me the tools to gradually take those experiences out of the equation. They did not go away, but I could manage them.

My ability to engage with a diverse set of people grew. Why? Well, I believe that when we get better at listening to ourselves, we get better at listening to others.

To sum it all up: For me, daily journaling was and is a life-altering tool. It is my anchor in stormy times, and the sail I set when the winds are blowing in the right direction.

Daily journaling is not only relevant when you are down-and-out. It is just as useful when you are at the top of your game. Here's a story from another client, a star performer named Tim:

My anxiety over my performance had reached new heights. I felt too many factors beyond my control were working against me.

Then I was introduced to daily journaling. After just a few days, I started to realize what led me to feel this lack of control, such as not having a clear framework in place for how to solve a problem, how to structure my thoughts, or how to perform a task.

The feeling was also driven by not having control or transparency over the performance and delivery of my team members.

Recognizing this, I started to reflect on these situations, discuss them with colleagues, and make action plans to break down and analyze them so I could build a case repository for how to best deal with stress in different situations. I constantly update this library with new situations and refer to it whenever I feel stressed. I know I cannot always control what goes on outside, but daily journaling has taught me that I can always control what goes on inside my mind.

Daily journaling has also helped me to ruthlessly focus on the most critical goal of each day, and to make sure I bring distinct delivery on what really matters. I make sure that I focus my energy and capacity on things that matter by spending five minutes each day thinking about the next day; more important, I also make sure that I do not spend too much effort on things that do not matter that much. Making conscious decisions about where I spend my time has helped me reduce anxiety and stress since I know that I don't need to bring my A game to every situation. In some situations, it's perfectly fine to settle for a good-enough result.

So, what should you focus on in your daily journaling? The simple answer is, whatever is important to you. When you use the tools and principles in this book, journal about the results you are seeing (or not seeing). If you have longer-term goals, journal about your progress working toward them. If you want to change certain behaviors or your mindset, set a goal and journal about it. More specifically, ask yourself:

What am I grateful for? Reflecting on what you are grateful for is a simple, often discussed, but unfortunately too-little-used way of strengthening your systems thinking (your ability to understand how things are connected) so you can see the deeper meanings of things in your life. Write down two or three things every day. Continuously reflecting on what you are grateful for also reduces your risk of depression and anxiety, increases your enthusiasm and optimism, improves your sleep, lowers your blood pressure, and enhances your ability to establish deep relationships.[2]

Furthermore, the habit of looking for what makes you feel proud and grateful builds the neurons associated with those emotions, so over time it will be easier for you to feel pride and gratitude and hence have a more positive outlook on yourself and your context. The objects of your gratitude can be as simple as being healthy, having a family, having a job, and so on. They do not have to be extraordinary (although you will for sure experience those things, too, if you apply the methods in this book).

What emotion or emotions have I felt the most strongly today? Labeling emotions, especially negative ones, is important, since it leads to relief. Research shows that when people are emotionally aroused, simply describing their emotional state in a word or two reduces activity in the part of the brain that controls emotions. Suppressing emotions, on the other hand, never works and can backfire. You may look normal on the outside, but the emotional activity in your brain may intensify. If you don't identify the emotion to yourself, it can easily be reawakened the next day.

What about positive emotions? Well, describing them in

a word or two can lead to positive affirmations. It makes it easier to relive them the next day, as well.

What mistakes did I make today that I will try to avoid in the future? Writing down the mistakes you made can reduce their number by as much as 50 percent, based on my experiences with clients. The reasons are that (1) what you write down you tend to remember; and (2) if you know that you are expected to write down your mistakes, you will pay more attention to what you are doing and make fewer of them.

What were my key dialogues and meetings today? You can keep track of them in a table like this:

With whom about what	What worked well	What I can improve

Few things stress us as much as other people, especially when we feel we are not relating well to them or collaborating effectively. Keeping score in this way helps us grow our skills in understanding people and hence forming and sustaining productive relationships with them.

8

Visit Your "Green Zone" Every Day

Moderately demanding to implement in your work life

We are basically built the same way as our ancient ancestors, who used to walk ten miles a day in search of food. Most of us today live far from that high level of physical activity.

Unfortunately, that makes us prone to disease and poor mental health, which multiple studies over the years have shown. One study showed that people who spent less than two and a half hours a week in moderate physical activity had a greater incidence of major health problems compared to those who undertook more than that—for example, 41 percent greater mortality, 43 percent increase in coronary heart disease, and 85 percent increase in colon cancer. The World Health Organization's recent study of two hundred thousand people showed that not exercising is worse than smoking.

In contrast, engaging in regular physical activity has multiple benefits: it makes you less anxious and/or depressed, it lowers your blood pressure and bad cholesterol, and it improves the flow of blood to your brain.

A typical day for a Navy SEAL team begins with a meeting to discuss what's on the day's agenda. Then the members either split up or visit their "Green Zone" as a team. The Green

Zone is their favorite physical activity—running, swimming, or whatever else they like to do.

During the Green Zone, they don't think about anything in particular; instead, they let their unconscious minds wander over past experiences, today's agenda, their life situations and priorities. This works as a mind cleansing, which energizes them but also makes them smarter, because physical activity grows new brain cells in the areas of the brain that are focused on learning. Also, the unconscious mind has access to our whole mind, which means that it can create new combinations of brain content, allowing us to come up with new ideas and solutions. This is a weakness of our conscious mind, which tends to have tunnel vision; when we think about a problem, our conscious mind tends to select only the pieces of information that seem directly related to it.

Research shows that people who are presented with a complicated problem with a lot of data and are forced to make a decision immediately afterward make worse decisions than those who first study the data, are distracted by something else, and then make their decision.[1] The reason? Brain scans show that the second group's unconscious minds continued to work on the problem while their conscious minds were focused on something else.

Ideally, your Green Zone should be two hours of physical exercise every day, which for most is impossible. Fortunately, science shows that thirty minutes a day is good enough. You can even break it up into three ten-minute blocks. Taking a ten-minute brisk walk before an important meeting gives you up to ninety minutes of extra energy, provides you with greater ability to focus, and burns off excess stress hormones.

So, try to visit your Green Zone every day. And why not do it like the SEALs—meet with your team or a colleague, then visit the Green Zone together.

9

Deliver Fully on All Deadlines with Bulletproof Results

Moderately demanding to implement in your work life

It is surprising to me how frequently professionals miss the deadlines they commit to. To make matters worse, they often don't warn you when they're going to be late. This leads to major disruptions since usually many stakeholders depend on their work to meet their own goals and priorities.

Worse still, much of the work professionals do deliver is incomplete and/or filled with obvious errors. This is not just a burden on the people who were counting on it, but on the people who must correct it.

If you struggle meeting deadlines and delivering complete results, here are some principles you should apply:

Operate on the principle that all deadlines must be met and all promises kept. You will reap great benefits from always meeting your deadlines. This includes coming to meetings on time, and respecting the time allotted to each item on the agenda. This simple principle is the secret of many high-performing professionals' success, no matter what their rank.

Promptness leads to development because it demands constant consideration of what you have to do and how you should do it to meet your deadlines. You also become more careful in your estimation of how long a task will take. The same applies to keeping promises. Being dependable requires you to be careful about what you commit to, and to ensure that the person you have made promises to has the same understanding of what that promise entails as you do.

Keep people informed of problems. If something happens that could potentially threaten a deadline, discuss that with the concerned stakeholders.

Discuss conflicts about deadlines. If you don't agree with a deadline set by a stakeholder, proactively explain your thinking and set a new deadline that you can both agree to.

Proactively discuss work quality. If you don't fully understand the quality of work results that a stakeholder requires, ask the stakeholder explicitly.

Plan all tasks before execution. Ask yourself questions like these:

- What is the bigger context of the task in its business implications and the people involved?
- How can I maximize the value of what I create?
- How can I make this task more interesting and enjoyable?
- How can I increase my overall efficiency in this task?
- How can I divide the task into steps, and how much time should I allocate to each of them?
- What challenges will each step present to my ability to execute it with maximum precision, efficiency, value, and enjoyment while meeting the deadline?
- What questions should I ask myself to stress-test my thinking?
- Do I need to get support from someone, and if so, why? Do I need to change how I perform certain subtasks, and if so, which, why, and how? Do I need to innovate and develop the tools I use, and if so, which, why, and how?

10

Define Your Most Important Goals for Every Workday

Moderately demanding to implement in your work life

In the best of all worlds, this is the method you should start with since it is the most effective and fastest way to rewire your brain for FEO. But since your brain is likely wired to support activity-focused behavior, this method could be too demanding at first. It is so powerful because it offers an integrated way to leverage four of the five cognitive elements of exciting outcome-focused behavior: (1) being passionate about creating a beautiful end product, (2) constantly challenging and competing with yourself, (3) cultivating deliberate expectations of the emotional experience you want, and (4) being able to monitor your progress, both while performing and after.

Creating your daily goals is not complicated. There are six simple steps:

1. During your weekly planning session, look at the coming week in your calendar.
2. For *each workday*, select one or two events/tasks as your daily goals. Simply by defining your goals clearly, you

activate your unconscious mind to get working on them, helping you be better prepared when it comes time to execute. These daily goals can be tasks that you:

    a. Need to perform better or more effectively

    b. Find uncomfortable or boring

    c. Will be managing for the first time

    d. Know are important to your boss, colleagues, or other stakeholders

    e. Believe are important for your longer-term goals and aspirations

3. Define an aspirational and exciting outcome for each task that forces you to do something different when you prepare or execute.

4. Devise tactics for how to execute on the daily goal that will push you closer to your desired outcome. This allows you to develop and learn, even if you don't actually achieve the outcome.

5. After you have executed, evaluate to what extent you achieved your outcome, focusing on what didn't work.

6. When you repeat the task, focus on the components that did not work and think about what you want to do differently.

Here is an example from one of my clients:

Day: Friday, February 18

What is the daily goal?	Improve the outcome of my biweekly meeting with my boss.
What is the aspirational and exciting outcome I want?	I want my boss to finally agree that we should change how we interact with the sales department. I have tried to achieve this for the past two months without success.

Tactics: What do I need to do better or differently to achieve that outcome?	In my previous attempts, I suspect I did not have a coherent enough story to pitch with sufficient documentation. This time, I will prepare a one-pager that clearly outlines the pros and cons of my proposal, and I will make sure to explain exactly how we execute the change. In addition, I will start the meeting by asking my boss to reflect upon what is working well and less well in our interactions with the sales department, so that I make sure that I understand how my boss thinks about this.
Evaluation after performing the daily goal:	
Did I achieve my outcome?	Almost. She bought into the idea that we might need to change how we interact with the sales department but wants a more detailed plan for how to achieve it.
Did I follow my idea of what to do better or differently? What should I do better or differently next time?	Yes, and it is good to invite her to reflect before I start to give my ideas. But I should have had a detailed plan in hand. Now this whole process will take at least another two to four weeks to get off the ground.

Some Tips for Defining Your Exciting Outcomes

It is important that your daily goals be "good enough"—don't sweat making the absolute 100 percent best goals. Being a perfectionist overwhelms your brain with emotions and makes you feel out of control.

When you have selected an activity to turn into a daily goal, think through the questions below. These will help you see all aspects of the activity so you can home in on an outcome that excites you.

The only criterion you need for selecting a task for an exciting outcome and the tactics you will use to achieve it is that it be *something that you can do better than you usually do!* The point is to compete with yourself.

You can compete with yourself in any task in three dimensions:

1. Time: Can you perform the task faster than you usually do? If so, how long should the task and each subtask take to perform? Example: *Instead of using the usual sixty minutes to prepare the material for the meeting with my boss on how my project is going, I want to spend forty minutes but achieve the same level of quality of the material.*

2. Quantity: Can you increase the output when you perform the task but without adding time? Example: *While I prepare the material for the meeting with my boss, I also want to create a first version of the same type of material to be shared with my colleagues in the project.*

3. Quality: What level of perfection in the end result would stretch and excite me? For example, can I perform the task without making any mistakes? What is the feeling I want to have when performing the task? What is the reaction I want from people when they see me perform the task or see my end result? Example: *I want my boss to say, "Stefan, this is without comparison the best material you have ever prepared for our meetings!"*

Another set of questions you should ask yourself is *If I perform this task better, what are the direct and indirect benefits for*

- our customers?
- our organization as a whole?
- each department that depends on this task?
- my manager and my colleagues?
- my own development?

To define your tactics for achieving your exciting outcome, you should think through the following questions:

- How should I execute the task?
- In what order should I execute the related subtasks?
- How should I execute each subtask?
- Are there things I should avoid when I execute?

Also, think about the way you have performed this task in the past and focus on how and what to change when you execute it. *Concentrate on what is challenging and exciting.* For example, if the task you've chosen is to conduct a meeting, think about the following:

- How have I generally performed in meetings recently? In which areas have I performed well and in which less well? What challenges me and makes me feel excited in meetings?
- How have I performed in this specific type of meeting? Which parts of my performance have worked well, and which have worked less well? Which have challenged me and made me feel excited?
- What are the two or three things I might change or add to how I behave to get closer to my desired outcome?
- How, in practice, will I do these two or three things during the meeting?
- What preparation is required for me to succeed in doing them in the way I have laid out?

Forcing yourself to think systematically improves your chances of getting close to your exciting outcome.

Furthermore, your development and mastery will increase if you make a habit of writing down what you learned when you performed your daily goals, by answering these four questions:

- Did I achieve my desired outcome?
- Did I stick to my approach?
- What did I learn?
- What would I do differently next time?

Use Your Daily Goals the Same Way an Athlete Prepares for a Game

Let's say you have a big presentation coming up in three weeks. Identify a handful of calendar events every week leading up to the big presentation and turn them into daily goals that allow you to practice your presentation skills. The topics do not have to be the same as the one for your big presentation; what matters is your results.

Use Daily Goals to Lift Your Spirits When You Are Feeling Down

When we are unhappy, our brain's default instruction is withdrawal; we just want to sit and do nothing and either wait for the low mode to pass or try to think ourselves out of it. Unfortunately, that only leads to an even lower mode since our Default Mode Network, the part of our brain where we think about our past and future, becomes overactive and we begin to ruminate. The proper medicine is to do the opposite and use FEO to get ourselves moving again. This pushes us into the present moment, activating our executive network (where our most important brain skills are hosted, e.g., decision-making). During and after any FEO-directed activity we feel more capable and thus better about ourselves. It doesn't have to be anything extraordinary. I always tell my clients, if you are low on energy and motivation, your daily goal might simply be "In the morning I will sort my emails in terms of urgent to answer and less urgent to answer by lunchtime." This seemingly simple and non-ambitious FEO is enough for you to get a sense of accomplishment and thus feel more energized.

When we do the same things in the same ways day in and day out, we quickly become bored with ourselves and what we do. We also tend to make more mistakes. Routine makes us "mindless." Csikszentmihalyi's research shows that we feel most alive when we are engaging our mental capacities in activities such as problem-solving. Actively defining a new goal for a routine task is a bulletproof way to fight boredom as well as to reduce your potential mistakes. Simply stretch your desired outcome in a way that forces you to think how you can perform the task in a new and different way, for example by exercising brutal and deliberate time-boxing. If a routine task normally takes you an hour, try cutting the time you allot to it to thirty minutes. This will force you to think in terms of outcomes and to devise a new way to execute it. After you have executed the task in the new way, you can evaluate your performance and learn. Another approach is to keep the time it takes to perform the familiar, comfortable, or boring task the same, but to radically raise the bar in output or quality. Either will help you develop and offer you a more exciting experience.

Here is one example from my own life: I hate housecleaning! It's boring, but it has to be done. Since I find it so boring, my brain works slower when I'm doing it, which makes it take even longer. To make it more interesting, I set myself the goal of faster completion times and devised new tactics to achieve it, by which I mean how I would clean and in what order I would do the rooms.

This approach changed everything. I was no longer focused on cleaning but on whether I was executing according to my plan and how well it was working. Competing with myself and stretching myself in this way made the task, if not exactly pleasurable, much more interesting. Plus, I learned a lot about cleaning, which in itself made the task less boring. When we know more about a topic or a task, we tend to enjoy it more because of our psychological need to experience "mastery."

Use the Daily Goals Method to Overcome Your Scars and Traumas

Many of my clients have suffered traumas—indelibly painful memories that trigger fight, freeze, or flight reactions.

Trauma has a sound and healthy function, which is to remind us to avoid similar events or situations in the future. We cannot erase a trauma. So, your key focus must be on how to manage it.

Since our minds scan our environment to make sense of what we are experiencing based on our past experiences, the original traumatic event is one of the more influential filters it has. That makes the trauma constantly present. Worse still, the mind inflates the similarities between the original trauma and the things that remind us of it.

Let's say you had a terrible meeting in a conference room at your office, where you felt humiliated and ridiculed. Walking past that conference room today, or just thinking about it, is triggering, as can be interactions with the people who were at that meeting. The mere thought of them can trigger a fight-or-flight reaction, as can other people whom your mind interprets as being similar to them.

You can't eliminate the trauma, but you can deflate it by proactively identifying the events and experiences that you face that are likely to trigger it. Use the Daily Goals method to define your tactics and set your desired outcomes. If you had a bad experience in a conference room, define an outcome that would help to neutralize it. This could be just to act differently this time around, or to focus your attention on something that will distract you when you are being triggered. Using Daily Goals in this way will reeducate your mind to identify the similarities between the original event and your present and future events and experiences more accurately. If you are triggered, you will know what is happening and why and be able to moderate your reaction.

The Multiple Benefits of the Daily Goals Method

Pursue one to two daily goals every day and

- **your brain will rewire itself** and start to see the world in terms of exciting outcomes and tactics.
- **you will be less sensitive** to external feedback and more prone to view it in a balanced way, based on both your own increased awareness of your performance and how others perceive it.
- **your sense of achievement will grow.** Often, especially when stressed, we can get the feeling that we have achieved nothing. Daily goals help you cultivate a thought pattern that says, "Well, I might not have done all the things I planned to do today, but what I did, I did really well."
- **you will sleep better.** One of the reasons we don't sleep well is because we have no clear goals or priorities for our upcoming day, which causes our unconscious to dwell instead on the challenges we face. Setting clear goals for tomorrow allows you to relax.
- **you will enhance your focus and attention as well as your overall memory and learning.** Your mind will be more attentive both before and after you execute your tasks, since

FEO behavior activates the effort-driven reward circuit in your brain. This will in turn increase how much you remember from your day as well as what you learn from executing your tasks.

- **you will become more persistent and "long-term."** Setting daily goals strengthens your indirect reward system by forcing you to think about both the short- and long-term impacts of getting something done.

The Power of Daily Goals

I worked with Monica, an administrator who works in public education. In addition to improving her work outcomes, she used the Daily Goals method to quit smoking. "What I think is probably the greatest gift of this method," she told me, "is how it enabled me to build and maintain a high level of motivation. What I have learned is that it is not the goals that are the prime source of motivation, but the process of setting outcomes and tactics, defining the approach, and evaluating the results. It is almost like detective work, in that you define your problem and then figure out how to solve it. More than anything, I think it was the challenge of solving the problem, rather than the benefits of not smoking, that kept me motivated."

Here are a few other testimonials from clients:

- "After just a few days of working with Daily Goals, I realized that I have at most operated on thirty percent of my potential. Most of the things I did were based on habit, without much attention to details or actual results. Daily Goals makes every day more meaningful and fun. Working with Daily Goals should be as natural as brushing your teeth." (Larry, chairman of the board, financial services company)

- "For some reason, I sense that everything I do during the day becomes more focused. I feel more attentive to what really happens." (Nina, chief of staff, manufacturing company)
- "For me, the real gift of having a daily goal is that I have accelerated my self-awareness. Being up-front in thinking about the challenges involved in my daily goal has taught me a lot about what I used to try to avoid, which means that I was not truly expanding my skills. Thinking through the challenges makes them easier to understand and overcome." (Brett, chief financial officer, utilities company)

Here's how one athlete, an Olympic hockey goalie, described her experience with daily goals:

I think I share two traits with other athletes: the never-ending striving to find smarter ways to improve, and the mental stress of knowing there are so many things I need to improve. These two traits create an ongoing inner game that you just need to master and win.

The mental stress can easily put you in a situation where you spread yourself too thin and try to address too many improvement areas at the same time, which generates even more mental stress since you then tend to ask yourself whether you are developing fast and tangibly enough.

Working with daily goals has helped me with this mental challenge. I can break down and evaluate all my longer-term goals and improvement areas in a concrete and insightful way daily. This gives me peace of mind and a sense that I am progressing in a tangible way. Furthermore, thinking about aspirational and exciting outcomes and tactics has made me much more aware of the decisive details in each of my improvement areas, details that I just need to nail to accelerate my development and performance.

Do I perform better in practice and in games with daily goals? For sure. Winning the inner game helps me perform at the level I desire.

11

Set Weekly or Monthly Stretch Goals for Skill Development and Effectiveness

Demanding to implement in your work life

When you feel that you have mastered the Daily Goals method and it has become part of your everyday routine, you are ready for the next step: to set a stretched, longer-term goal or exciting outcome beyond what you want to achieve during a day. Here I recommend that you still use time frames such as a week or a month as opposed to years. This is because the shorter the time frame, the easier it is to define a clear and tangible FEO and create a concrete step-by-step plan to achieve it.

Longer-term goals that require you to repeatedly stretch outside your comfort zone accelerate learning and innovation, such as if you want to radically improve a skill, build a new skill fast, or deliver a project much faster than such projects are usually delivered. The mindset stretched goals require is similar to that of superstar athletes, who, to accelerate their development, are constantly setting targets that are well beyond their current capabilities.

Important: if you set weekly or monthly stretch goals, link your daily goals and most important tasks to them when you do your daily journaling and learning.

Let's say I develop a stretched-development target for my coaching practice and define it as "to radically improve the effectiveness and client value of my practice." One of my monthly exciting outcomes would be to focus on the number of clients I can manage simultaneously.

Suppose I currently manage twenty clients, and let's say I define a monthly exciting outcome as "to increase the number of clients I can manage effectively from twenty to twenty-five." This goal is reasonable and gives me some psychological comfort for being doable. It is a good feeling, but I will most likely think incrementally about what I need to change and improve, which will put a cap on my actual results.

If I instead formulate the goal as "to increase the number of clients I can manage effectively from twenty to forty," something interesting and valuable happens in my head. I realize that I need to analyze and experiment with every aspect of my approach, for example, selection and time efficiency:

- Which criteria do I apply for selecting clients?
- How do I spend my time across my current client portfolio? Why?

I could also evaluate which elements of the coaching model are not working effectively for me, for example:

- Up-front assessment of the client's capabilities and mindset
- Creating the client's business and development goals
- Selecting tangible actions to achieve those goals
- Evaluation of progress and corrective actions
- Effectiveness of my own and the client's preparation for coaching sessions
- Effectiveness of coaching sessions per coaching channel, such as physical meetings, Skype meetings, phone meetings, email exchanges, or messaging
- Effectiveness of time distribution and channel mix

As a result of that analysis, I will likely be forced to look outside my current approach. This leads me to ask questions like:

- Are there smart tools, such as apps, I can use to make my coaching more effective?
- Can I create peer apprenticeship teams of clients, that is, would any of my current clients benefit from working with each other to support their further development and growth?

The point here is not whether I should be able to manage forty clients, but how an ambitious stretch goal demands that I become much smarter to potentially achieve it.

12

Pull All Four Levers for Success to Achieve What Most People Would Consider Impossible

Demanding to implement in your work life

Most professionals struggle in working toward their dreams, or what they or others around them regard as almost impossible to achieve. Of the many reasons for this, the main one is that they do not set their sights high enough and so fail to pull all four levers for success. These are:

1. Identify and mobilize people who can reward, support, and teach you.
2. Think continuously about how to tweak your environment, your activities, and your situations to better enable you to work toward what you want to achieve.
3. Make sure that every step you take is rewarding by using the Daily Goals method to make the work exciting.
4. Proactively identify and manage everything that could potentially distract or deter you from working toward what you want to achieve. This includes making a list of people that you need to avoid—and then avoiding them.

To show you that an intentional approach such as this can work, I want to share two of my clients' success stories.

From Feared Smart Guy to Admired People Leader in Less Than Twenty-Four Months

Jim was a sales director at a global company when I met him in the fall of 2016. The CEO of the company had brought me in to help Jim develop his people skills so he could be a candidate to replace the CEO when he stepped down within the next two to three years. The brief I got from the CEO was that Jim was smart and business savvy but often impossible to work with.

Jim and I had our first meeting at his office early one morning. The first question I asked him was how he viewed his work and the people he worked with. Without any hesitation Jim responded that his work was fun but that he was surrounded by two types of people: smart people and idiots. I then asked him about his aspirations and dreams. He said that he wanted to become a CEO of a public company. My follow-up question was if he understood the requirements for a CEO position, particularly the ability to mobilize diverse groups of people around a strategy and create strong support and trust throughout the organization. Jim responded vaguely, but he clearly understood that this was an important ability for anyone who aspired to the role.

Then I zoomed in on his view of people as being either smart or idiots and asked him if he thought that was a viable perspective for a would-be CEO, given what we had just discussed. Jim sat quietly for a while. Then he said, "I guess I have some serious work to do in how I think about and deal with people."

We agreed that a good way to start our work together would be to gather feedback from a large and diverse group of people on how they viewed Jim and his strengths and development needs. The responses I got were crystal clear:

Everyone said that Jim was a smart guy, but that he was limited in the types of people he respected and worked well with. If Jim didn't like you, he made that painfully clear. Some of the people I talked to told me they dreaded their meetings with him.

After that, Jim and I focused on the specifics of his people management, from how he prepared for and behaved in meetings, to problems he had with certain colleagues and subordinates. I showed him ways to create concrete development plans for his direct reports, and how to coach and guide them. In addition, I shared relevant nuggets of behavioral science and neuroscience with him, for example, how the mind processes information and how to assess people's motivations and thinking patterns.

As we continued to meet, the way Jim talked about his colleagues changed. He became much more able to focus on their strengths. Step-by-step, he developed productive ways to work with all of them, and his ability to quickly establish effective collaboration with people he'd just met increased.

After twenty-two months, the CEO announced his retirement, and Jim was tapped as a candidate for the role. I did another set of 360-degree feedback interviews for his further development, but also as potential input for the board when they evaluated him. I reinterviewed everyone I'd talked to before and added several more to get as broad and deep a feel as possible, for a total of twenty-nine. The results were fascinating. The key theme of every interview was that Jim had dramatically changed. His smarts were still there, but what stood out now was his ability to deal constructively with all kinds of people, and to help his employees flourish and grow. "He is not the same person. The development as a leader he has managed to achieve is mind-blowing," one said. "I don't know how he has been able to do it."

Jim got the CEO position, and we have continued to work together since. I asked Jim to describe his journey, and he told me:

How did I transform myself? I think several things made it possible. The first was the insight that the path I was on as a leader would not take me to where I wanted to go, which was to become CEO. Until I could work well with all types of people in the company, I would not get there. I can remember the room I was sitting in when this insight came to me.

The second thing was self-insight, that is, understanding *why* I was acting and thinking the way I was about the people around me. When I started working on my people-management skills, I realized that throughout my career I had taken great pride in always making the best and smartest assessments of everything, including people. Being the smartest guy in the room had been very important to me. I realized that was something I had to change.

The third thing was getting support. I had support from my boss, my wife, and my coach, which meant I had daily reminders of what I needed to do to become a people-oriented leader—and daily opportunities to discuss my efforts to meet that goal.

The fourth thing was to change my environment so it would force me to focus on my people skills. One thing I did was book frequent one-on-one meetings with my team members so we could discuss how they felt about their situations, what was working for them and what wasn't, and so on. Another was to spend more time with a team member who was struggling. My original plan had been to let him go, but I decided to really invest in him instead, both to help him perform better but also as an opportunity to push myself to become better at understanding and developing people different from myself. In addition, I created a few people-oriented processes in my team to keep the development of my people skills high on my agenda. One thing I did was to make sure that all team members wrote me detailed feedback memos twice a year in which they critiqued my leadership. I also wrote them twice-yearly memos about their achievements, strengths, and development needs.

The fifth thing was probably the most important. Early on, the development journey itself became my purpose and focus, not my ambition to become CEO. I enjoyed every step I took, since the steps gave me so many benefits. All of a sudden, I saw other people's uniqueness in terms of both their strengths and their development needs, which helped me understand how I could help them enjoy what they did more and add more value to the company. Being more able to appreciate other people's opinions, perspectives, and experiences enriched my thinking.

Learning to Speak a Foreign Language in Eight Weeks

Clarita is a client of mine who works for a large private equity firm. When I first met her, I was surprised to learn that she was fluent in Swedish. When I asked her how she learned the language, she told me this amazing story, which shows how important deliberation and planning are to reach a stretched goal:

I had just moved to Sweden from the US to start a new job. I had never been to Scandinavia before and had no knowledge of Swedish. When I interviewed for the job, they'd told me that language would not be an issue, as everyone spoke English.

The first meeting I went to was an all-staff meeting. I had expected it to be conducted in English, but I was quite wrong. Everyone spoke Swedish and I did not understand a single word. Afterward, one of the partners of the firm introduced himself to me and said, "I would suggest that you set yourself a deadline to learn our language. What about you start speaking Swedish by October fifteenth?"

It was August 14 that day. Looking back now, the partner was probably trying to encourage me, but he was also making a joke. Whatever it was, it had an incredibly motivating effect on me. I thought, "This guy thinks I can't do it? I'm going to show him!"

I hired a language tutor to work with me for an hour twice a week. I told her my goal was to be able to work in Swedish by October 15. She laughed, but quickly realized that I was dead serious.

The first step was that I refused to speak any other language than Swedish with my tutor and in all nonwork situations—for example, at the grocery store, in taxis, leaving and picking up the kids at the day care. The people I was struggling to talk to could switch to English if they liked, but I continued responding in my broken Swedish.

After a while, when I felt like I was able to speak simple sentences, I expanded my safety zone to include my assistant at work. She could switch to English as much as she wanted, but I stubbornly responded in Swedish.

The third step was switching to Swedish at work generally. Here I used my tutor a lot. I tested my presentations and other work-related communications on her before I brought them to my teams.

Starting to work in Swedish happened gradually. I did, though, from October 15 on, always speak to the specific partner who'd challenged me in Swedish and never switched to English in any of the internal meetings.

The first thing that stands out in both of these stories is what I regard as one of the most important levers for goal fulfillment: *other people's support!* Seek out people who teach you what you need to know to reach your goals, push you to stay focused on your goals, and celebrate with you when you make progress. You want to be around people who are good at what you want to become good at or are good at achieving the results that you want to achieve. As kids, we all understood this. We had teachers, coaches, and friends who supported, rewarded, and coached us.

The second is the deliberate thinking. What activities and situations would be relevant for you to pursue? How can you reshape your environment so that it forces you to think about and work toward your goal? Do you need to add activities, situations, habits, or practices, or can you simply tweak your current activities?

Third is the importance of feeling rewarded every step of the way. No matter how important the goal is, if you don't experience the steps you take as rewarding in themselves, you will not continue to work toward it. Daily goals are essential to make this happen.

The fourth thing that stands out is a deep understanding of what could distract or deter you from working toward your goal. Is it how you think about yourself? Is it your current habits or skills? Is it your previous experiences? Is it other competing priorities? Are there people currently in your life who will deter you?

The last question is particularly important if your goal is

to change your behavior, because human beings are wired to punish people who break behavioral norms. So, if you are hanging out with people who would not like your changed behavior, don't hang out with them!

In conclusion, if you want to live your dream, make sure you pull all four of those levers.

When You Think You Have "Too Much to Do"— Don't Prioritize

Demanding to implement in your work life

I hesitated at first when I thought about including a chapter on prioritization. Why? One reason is that when you have rewired your brain to master FEO, prioritization will not be an issue.

But I decided to include it anyway simply because of all the hysteria in the workplace around having "too much to do." So, I will tell you again: Stop thinking that you can't pursue everything on your agenda without extra resources or help. That is simply not the case. Start with the understanding that the time is there for those who commit to using it better. Once you have cultivated this mindset, the work to figure out how to do this successfully begins.

I will use myself as an example. At any point, I am working with thirty-plus clients. I coach about a third of them weekly, another third biweekly, and the last third monthly. All these client sessions, plus the required prep work, means that my calendar is crammed.

All my clients work in dynamic professional environments in which new problems, challenges, and opportunities continuously arise, often interfering with our scheduled time. The other morning, one of my clients, a CFO, called me and said, "Stefan, I just got notice from a board member that the CEO is leaving the company and the board wants to consider me for the position. I am really excited about this opportunity and wonder if you could interview some of my stakeholders? I would use the results to support my application."

I asked her how many interviews she wanted me to carry out and when she would need the results. She answered, "I have twenty-six stakeholders in mind. Could I have the result in three weeks?"(!) The large number of stakeholders made sense, given that it is a global company, but my gut reaction to the deadline was "This is impossible. Helping her with this will take at least thirty hours. How on earth am I going to fit this in?"

The primitive part of my mind wanted to say, "No, I can't help you, this is impossible." But I have rewired my mind so that whenever my gut says, "This is impossible," my trained reaction kicks in: "This is an interesting situation. Perhaps I have some development opportunities to pursue here?" I told the client I would see what I could do and call her back within an hour.

Since I practice what I preach, my whole life is in my calendar. As I looked over the next three weeks of entries, I asked myself these questions:

- *Are there any tasks I can postpone?* I am generally hesitant to go down this path because you risk building a big backlog of tasks, which creates stress and anxiety, and runs counter to my ambition to be flexible and offer a high level of service. But I did find one task that was important but not at all time critical. This freed up approximately three hours.

- *Which of these tasks can I execute in a smarter and faster way?* This is a much more profitable path to pursue than the first, since it leads to development. I identified fourteen tasks that I felt I could perform more efficiently, which bought me another eight hours.
- *Can I pursue the feedback interviews and the work around them in a more efficient way?* This is an important question and a great opportunity to spot areas of potential improvement. Typically, I plan these 360-degree feedback interviews well in advance, which means I schedule them myself. This takes some time, probably fifteen minutes per interviewee, what with mailing and texting back and forth. If I got the client's assistant to book them instead, that would save me fifteen minutes for each of the twenty-six interviews, or six and a half hours. Another area I considered was the thirty minutes I usually allot to each interview. Most actually take less time. So, I decided that I should only schedule twenty minutes for each interview, which would save me 26 x 10 minutes, or 4.3 hours.
- What about my time budget, which is usually fifty-five hours a week? I decided to add three hours to it per week, which gave me an additional nine hours.

Now my time investment was about twenty hours (fifteen hours to do all the interviews, one hour to compile them into a single document, two hours to do my analysis of the feedback, and two hours to discuss the feedback with my client). With all the other time I'd saved, plus the three extra hours per week of work, I could easily accomplish this impossible task.

The next three weeks were packed, but I was able to send my client the final document one day early. The next day we had our debrief. How did I feel when we finished? Like Superman! I had overcome my own kryptonite, which was my gut reaction that the task was impossible.

Nothing is impossible if you take the time to think about how to do it.

Shape Your Destiny

Evolve Your Mindset to Become
the Superstar You Can Be

When FEO behavior becomes a daily habit, you'll have learned how to love everything you want or need to do. Now you can take the next step, which is to unlock your unlimited potential to become the superstar you can be. To do that you need to evolve the only asset you can truly control: your mind or mindset. Because how you think about yourself will shape your destiny. Remind yourself of this every day!

Our mindset is made up of all our conscious and unconscious beliefs and expectations about what is possible, and hence what we should aspire to, what priorities we should set, and what kinds of people we are drawn to. When you visualize your mindset in a clear and tangible way as a set of beliefs and think them through, you activate the most powerful part of your brain, your unconscious mind.

Your unconscious mind is an extraordinary information-processing engine that works 24–7 to help you observe what goes on around you and make quick decisions based on your beliefs—often before you are aware that you are doing so. As mentioned earlier, the unconscious mind has access to our whole mind, which means that it can create new combinations of brain content, allowing us to come up with new ideas and solutions. It can also continue to work on a problem even when you decide to stop working on the problem to focus your conscious mind on something else.

Furthermore, recent research around mindset suggests that our conscious and unconscious beliefs and expectations influence not just our personalities but our physiology.

To prove this, the psychologists Alia J. Crum and Ellen J. Langer asked eighty hotel maids how much they exercised.[1] Most said they didn't exercise regularly, and more than a third reported not getting any exercise at all, even though they cleaned an average of fifteen rooms a day. Changing linens for fifteen minutes burns forty calories, vacuuming for fifteen minutes burns fifty calories, cleaning bathrooms for fifteen minutes burns sixty calories, and so on for other housekeeping tasks.

The researchers checked the hotel maids' body weight, body fat, and blood pressure. Then they divided them into two groups. One group returned to work as usual. The second group spent some time with the researchers, who told them how many calories they typically burned in their working day, which more than met the CDC's recommendations for an active lifestyle. After four weeks the researchers checked the body weight, body fat, and blood pressure of the two groups. Although their behavior had not changed, the second group's average weight, blood pressure, body fat, waist-to-hip ratio, and body mass indexes had changed for the better.

What a fascinating result! But that is just one example of the monumental power of our thoughts. For example, if you visualize a potentially difficult event in the future—a meeting with a colleague who often makes you feel stressed, for example—your thoughts can evoke exactly the same painful physical reactions that you are anticipating! In this case, the brain doesn't distinguish between imagination and reality—it simply reacts. For a less charged example of this phenomenon, if you imagine that a dog has entered the room, your brain reacts in exactly the same way as if a dog had actually come into the room.

A fascinating demonstration of the power of thought is an experiment that the abovementioned psychologist Ellen J. Langer conducted in 1979 with a group of men in their eighties.[2] Langer took over a monastery and decorated it to look as if it were 1959, when the men were twenty years younger. She further stocked it with newspapers and LPs from 1959 and screened movies from the era.

Then she divided the participants into two groups. The experimental group would move into the monastery and live and act as much as possible as they had in 1959. The control group would only talk about how they lived in 1959.

All of the men's physical and mental capacities were tested, both before and after the experiment. All of them had become somewhat "younger" in areas such as weight, gait, and posture, but among the experimental group, 63 percent improved their intelligence (as compared to 44 percent of the control group). The experimental group also showed improvements in their mobility and manual dexterity—even their arthritis diminished. What is even more incredible is how long the experiment lasted: it took only one week to achieve these benefits.

Those were only minor shifts in mindset and they had major results. Now imagine what a major shift in mindset could do for you.

Your Hypertalkative Inner Voice

Most professionals appreciate the importance of mindset, but struggle to shape theirs in a good way. Why? Because our mindsets are preconfigured. That preconfiguration is like a hypertalkative inner voice that constantly bombards us with bad ideas, incomplete thinking, unnecessary fears, and instructions that will distract us from unlocking our unlimited potential.

In his book *The Untethered Soul: The Journey Beyond Yourself,* the spiritual leader Michael A. Singer describes our preconfigured mind's ever-present activity:

> In case you haven't noticed, you have a mental dialogue going on inside your head that never stops. It just keeps going and going. Have you ever wondered why it talks in there? How does it decide what to say and when to say it? How much of what it says turns out to be true? How much of what it says is even important? And if right now you are hearing, "I don't know what you're talking about. I don't have any voice inside my head!"—that's the voice we're talking about.

Singer argues that you are not your mind, which has a life of its own. To liberate yourself from its negative influence, you need to learn how to take a step back and observe it.

Your inner voice is the product of the environment we humans lived in for most of the two hundred thousand years of our existence. In this primitive environment the availability of food and other provisions was seasonal and a constant challenge. Humans also lived with constant threats, such as dangerous animals and rival tribes.

Shaped by this environment, your inner voice is all about one thing: survival. Accordingly, it counsels you to take as little risk as possible, spend as little energy as possible, and (by any means possible) seem attractive in the eyes of others.

Your inner voice imposes numerous behaviors that are completely counterproductive for you to unlock your potential. When you are presented with an idea or a decision at work that you don't understand, it warns you away from it, saying, "What a stupid idea or decision. Who on earth came up with it?" It instructs you to divide your world into us and them and to avoid anyone who is different. It assigns only good attributes to "us" and bad attributes to "them," ensuring that you will stay in line with the shared opinions of your group, rather than make up your own mind. When you have problematic relationships, your inner voice presses you to bad-mouth the others behind their backs (your inner voice is a coward). As for your dreams and aspirations, it sees only risks and uncertainties and bombards you with doubt: "Can I really do this? No one else seems to be doing this. I better stick with what I know."

In its pursuit to minimize the energy you spend, your inner voice presses you to stick to what you already know and are good at, instead of building new knowledge and learning new skills. It urges you to take the easiest way to achieve a goal or perform an activity, even if that involves cheating or cutting corners. Mostly, it pushes you to focus on what you can't influence rather than what you can. Why? Because if you focus on what you can influence—yourself—you would need to expend a lot of energy.

When things go wrong, your inner voice urges you to feel sorry for yourself rather than to take charge and act to make things better, and to assign the blame to someone else. It tells you that talent is something that other people have, that you should be satisfied with watching Roger Federer and Serena Williams play tennis on TV rather than practicing to be as good as you can at something yourself. In its pursuit to make you appear attractive to others, your inner voice presses you to exaggerate your achievements when you talk about them, and to make promises that you know you can't keep.

Most of your bad behaviors, questionable feelings, and ridiculous thoughts have nothing to do with your personality, your upbringing, or your life experiences. Most of it is driven by that inner voice. You never asked to have that inner voice, so you can't blame yourself for the damage it's caused in your personal and professional life. But you can do something about it.

The first step is to realize who you really are. *You* have the power to reshape your brain to host any thought, feeling, skill, or behavior, and to create and pursue any of the unlimited possibilities your life offers. *You* are your dreams, your desire to learn and develop, and your appetite to explore the unknown. *You* are unlimited. Inside you is the embryo of someone who can make a unique contribution to the world—a Mozart, David Bowie, Ram Dass, Steve Jobs, Serena Williams, Martin Luther King, Oprah Winfrey, Albert Einstein, Lady Gaga, or anyone else you admire.

To unlock your inner star, stop believing in talent. If you believe that talent exists, you will avoid spending energy on things you believe you lack the talent to do. As far as I'm concerned, talent does not exist.

One of the things that makes me a good and effective coach is that I view all my clients as the potential superstars they are. Whatever clients want or need to achieve, I can envision them achieving it. This helps me to see the steps they need to take and what tools and approaches they need to learn. Furthermore, the conviction that talent does not exist fuels my clients with the courage to accept the many shortcomings and development areas I help them address to reach their dreams and aspirations.

This superfuel is readily available for you, too, if you think about yourself in the right way.

Unlock Your Unlimited Potential

To unlock your unlimited potential, improve how you think about problems and how to solve them. Problem-solving is fundamental for intrinsic motivation, well-being, development, and performance. As my mentor Mihaly Csikszentmihalyi discovered in his research on optimal human functioning, few things make us feel as alive and strong as when we are solving problems, and few things kill our motivation as much as facing problems we either can't understand or can't solve.

Most professionals go terribly wrong in problem-solving because of their inner voices.

"A famous bon mot asserts opinions are like assholes, in that everyone has one," the composer, musician, comedian, and actor Tim Minchin told the graduating class of the University of Western Australia in 2013. "There is great wisdom in this, but I would add that opinions differ significantly from assholes in that your opinions should be constantly and thoroughly examined."[3]

Obviously, it's better to maintain an objective viewpoint and reason logically about problems we encounter, but few things are harder for our inner voice to accept than observations, ideas, and facts that contradict our preexisting opinions—even though we instinctively sense that a contradiction almost always signals that potential new insights and knowledge can be gained. Not only do we have a hard time embracing contradictions, our inner voice becomes upset when we are exposed to them. Under certain circumstances, contrary evidence can impel us to cling to our beliefs all the harder.

Back in the late 1990s when I began my journey into neuroscience and the human mind, I was flabbergasted to learn how conservative the mind is about its biases; to preserve them, it frequently rejects new knowledge. To warn about this tendency, a McKinsey colleague and I spearheaded a project called the H-Files (the Human Files), which focused on the foibles of the human mind. It included this illustration:

The human mind is very conservative in accepting new knowledge

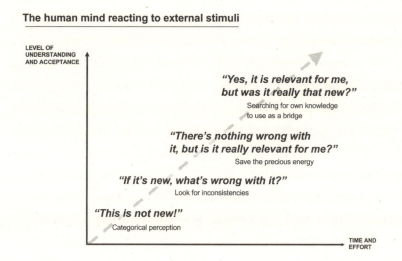

It was not scientific by any means, but I have showed it to thousands of people over the years. Most laugh and say, "Yeah, that is exactly what happens in my head when I am confronted with things that contradict what I believe."

First, we try to reject the contradiction by claiming the person raising it is an outsider or lacks qualifications, experience, or seniority. But the likelihood that you or someone who is exactly like you, with the same background, interests, qualifications, and experience, would come up with a contradiction—for example a completely new way of working—is low. The source is almost always someone from outside your group.

Second, your inner voice tries to sidestep the contradiction by claiming that you and your situation are unique. Hence, you claim that the contradiction—the new way of working—looks good but is not applicable to your unique situation.

Third, and as a last resort, your voice makes you a liar by making you declare that you already tried the proposed new way of working and it did not work.

Consultants often face these three tricks when they try to help an organization, but it also happens within companies. If one department executes a specific work process well and tries to share its technique with another department, the people in the other department will make use of all of these tricks to avoid having to learn a new way of working. In my early years as a consultant, I believed clients when they claimed that what we proposed was irrelevant or had already been tried, but it did not take me too long to figure out that they were lying.

Obviously, the contradiction could in fact be wrong. It could be a bad thing to pursue. But then again, it might not be.

Your Inner Voice Is Gullible

While your inner voice makes you resist new ideas, it also makes you extremely gullible. Just imagine the following scenario:

You are out walking and decide to get a coffee. The coffee shop you go into is crowded, but you manage to find a table. After a while, a guy comes up to you and asks if he can sit with you. He introduces himself and you begin to chat. You learn that he works as a salesman for a software company that specializes in advanced analytics and big data, and you sense that he is a nice guy who is good at what he does. All of a sudden, he changes the subject: "I got a call this morning from one of my friends. He has a friend whose friend has a work colleague, Mr. Stevenson, who has been missing for a while and is presumed dead by the authorities. I wonder how he died." No sooner does he tell you this than he looks at his watch, realizes he is late for a meeting, and rushes out of the coffee shop. As you finish your coffee, you can't stop thinking about Mr. Stevenson. How did he die? You start to break the problem down into all its aspects.

"Did he die of natural causes?" you ask yourself. "Perhaps he was murdered, or maybe he committed suicide." You summarize the alternatives: natural causes, murder, suicide. "Yeah," you think, "that sums up all the options."

But you are wrong! You have fallen prey to one of the biggest impediments to critical thinking there is: anchoring. Anchoring is a powerful cognitive bias that your inner voice has developed to facilitate quick and energy-efficient decision-making to keep you safe. It is ever present in how we perceive ourselves and the world. What it means is that the first piece of information we get about a problem or a situation tends to bias our subsequent thinking.

Your anchor in this situation is the question "I wonder how he died?" If you go back and think about what your new acquaintance said, you should spot one obvious aspect or option to the problem: nobody knows for certain that Mr. Stevenson is dead.

Remember that Mr. Stevenson is missing and only assumed to be dead by the authorities. This does not mean that he *is* dead. Is he missing because of his own actions? Was he kidnapped?

Another important aspect or option to consider, given the information you have, is counterintuitive: perhaps Mr. Stevenson is not dead because he never existed! Face it, you met a guy who shared some third- or fourth-hand information. You have no facts to suggest you should believe it.

Your new acquaintance seemed like a nice guy. But he could be a con man or a pathological liar. You trusted him because of another cognitive bias: we tend to trust people we can relate to. But nice-seeming people are not intrinsically more trustworthy than less nice-seeming people.

So always be aware of what your anchor is in any situation—and don't automatically assume that people who seem to be like you can be trusted. That's not always the case.

So keeping all that in mind, let's get started. In this section, I will provide you with tools and principles that can help you overcome that inner voice and embrace new knowledge, think more logically, and problem-solve more effectively.

14

Don't Participate in Negative Talk

Easy to implement in your work life

Negativity is the default setting in most of the organizations I have encountered. People commonly bad-mouth one another and complain about their jobs while displaying cynical attitudes toward management. The forces at work here emanate from weaknesses that most of us share through our inner voice: the unwillingness to take risks and face uncomfortable situations. So, instead of confronting people, we find it easier and safer to talk behind their backs. Your inner voice is fundamentally lazy, too, so instead of rethinking our tasks, we would rather complain about them. Complaining takes less energy than actually improving our situation. And finally, your inner voice has a huge need to feel important and seen. That is why our default reaction to decisions that other people make that affect us is disgust, anger, or some other kind of negativity.

Participating in negative talk at work will only distract you from your journey to becoming the superstar you can be. Furthermore, it will make you feel like a bad person. Deep down, we all know that complaining, gossiping, and bad-mouthing are wrong.

Here is what you need to do:

- Never share any conflicts or differences of opinion you have with a colleague with anyone except that colleague.
- If you're not going to work to solve your relationship issue, then stop thinking about it! It mustn't be that important.
- If someone approaches you to bad-mouth a colleague, refuse to participate. Encourage the person to discuss those differences with the other person.
- If anyone makes a decision you don't understand, don't judge it too quickly. Learn about its background and what it will mean in practice. You have a brain; use it.

Take these principles to heart. If you aspire to live by them, I promise you will experience a greater sense of inner peace and be viewed as a person of integrity.

15

Do Weekly Risk Assessment
and Contingency Planning

Easy to implement in your work life

The Navy SEALs invest a lot in risk assessment and contingency planning; they plan their missions meticulously. But they also have a saying that "no plan survives first contact with the enemy." They know that "shit happens"—that there will always be factors beyond their control or aspects of the situation that they did not think hard enough about.

Why is this relevant for you? Well, you don't want your inner voice to obsess or get caught in a spiral of negative thinking. But the more quality time you spend thinking about what could realistically go wrong, the better prepared you will be to deal with whatever comes up.

Following are some examples of common negative surprises that I have seen with clients:

- Key decisions are changed or not made.
- New tasks are introduced.
- Deadlines and requirements are changed.
- People don't do what they are supposed to.
- Key stakeholders disagree on issues.
- Collaborators fail to do their part.

Make it a weekly habit to think ahead and ask yourself, "What could go wrong?" You can then plan for those risks should they materialize.

From experience, I know that professionals who are in a good place seldom do risk assessments because they don't think they need to. If everything is going well, why focus on what could go wrong? It is almost as though thinking about bad things causes them emotional pain. I understand the psychology—it's a little like making contingency plans for your eventual divorce at the same time you are planning your wedding.

A few years back, I was counseling the CEO of a fast-growing biotech company on his mergers and acquisitions strategy. His company was awaiting approvals from regulators before it could promote certain aspects of its product's benefits in its marketing. An approval would also enable the company to strike a global distribution deal with a huge partner.

I frequently asked him about the approvals' progress, and the CEO insisted it was as good as in the bag. He even showed me some of the correspondence between his company and the regulators, which looked promising. But since I operate on the notion that nothing is done until it is done, I asked him on at least three occasions about his plan B. Each time, he almost got upset, but then laughed it off, saying, "Stefan, I appreciate your concern, but, honestly, I know how these regulators think and operate, and given our track record, this is a done deal."

Did his company get approval from the regulators? No.

Did the company have a contingency plan? No.

Did the CEO keep his job? No!

The point of risk assessment and contingency planning is that nothing is a done deal until it is a done deal, no matter how good things look. You can never control all the factors for success. You will always be dependent on other people and the ways that related and sometimes even unrelated events play out.

Risk management and contingency planning are equally important if you are struggling or have failed at something. One reason is to get a balanced view of the risks you are facing; when you are in a bad place, you tend to overestimate the likelihood of further failure, which can lead to analysis paralysis and inaction. Another reason is to become smarter about why you failed in the first place—what risks did you not take into consideration?

After starting to practice risk management weekly and daily, one of my clients said:

Before every week, and before every day, I reflect on the potential risks. For the risks that could potentially have big impact, I make implementation intentions, i.e., action plans for how to deal with the risk if it becomes reality. One of the main reasons why I felt stressed before I started to do risk management was because I knew that there always was a risk of "shit hitting the fan." By *proactively identifying risks and reducing the probability of their occurrence,* I feel much more in control; I always know that I have done my best to avoid the worst outcomes. But if risks do occur, I have a plan to manage them.

16

Don't Be the Victim—Be the Detective

Easy to implement in your work life

If prisoners of war can train their minds to withstand torture, you can manage your mind to have a better and more resilient life at work. The number one mindset to avoid is perhaps our default mindset as human beings: feeling like a victim.

The victim mindset helps us in the short term. If you are a victim of your circumstances, or of other people's actions and demands, you don't have to do anything about it; only the people who are making you miserable have the power to change your circumstances. Erase this way of thinking from your mental model. When you allow it into your world, you give yourself permission to feel helpless. That only makes things worse.

Instead, practice what I call the detective mindset. If someone is mean or difficult to work with, turn them into an interesting problem to solve. Make it your project to find out why this person behaves in this way, and how you can manage the person more effectively.

I can't count how many of my clients have suffered from poor relationships with their bosses or one or more of their colleagues and have seriously considered leaving their positions to pursue something else far away from those "bad people." This is a natural tendency since few things hurt us more emotionally and mentally than bad relationships. The problem is that the world is filled with difficult people. So, if you want to grow and shape your destiny, you need to master the skill of transforming seemingly unworkable situations into productive ones.

I tell my clients to take two or three weeks to observe their nemeses and try to figure out why they say and behave the way they do—and to consider what the clients themselves might say and do to trigger those bad behaviors. I urge them to experiment with different ways to interact with these others. Most of the time this works well, and some clients have in weeks been able to completely change the dynamics of these seemingly impossible relationships.

Here's a testimonial from one of them:

> I worked with a tough person who would often shoot down my suggestions and ideas without any real explanation. I could not figure out how to manage him, and I was becoming increasingly frustrated. Then the detective mindset was introduced to me, which replaces fear and emotions with intellectual curiosity. I began to probe this person about why he felt the way he did about the ideas and suggestions I brought to him, and what he would do differently if he were me. I studied his motivations and his decisions. Soon I concluded that he was under tremendous personal and professional pressure, which was affecting his ability to engage with me. Knowing this background changed my mindset; I realized that I needed to put myself in his shoes and first establish trust and credibility before jumping into my work with him. After I put my learnings into practice, he started to see me as a trusted colleague and adviser.

The detective mindset is relevant in all areas of your professional life, not just relationships. If you fail to reach a goal, feeling bad about it won't help you. The biggest problem with failure is not the failure itself but the emotional pain it creates, which inflates our perception of how big or severe the failure really is. The same is the case when we experience success—the emotional pleasure can easily make us overestimate ourselves. The trick, whether it is failure or success you are experiencing, is to quickly snap out of your emotional intoxication. Take an analytical approach to get a balanced and nonemotional view of the situation; that is, turn it into a learning opportunity: *Why did I not succeed? Did I set the wrong goal? Did I prepare poorly? Was my plan incomplete and not deliberate enough? Did my execution lack effort and conviction? What do I need to do differently next time?* Or conversely: *What did I do right? How can I do that again?*

Use the fifty-fifty principle, which one of my clients taught me, to think about your past, present, and future successes and failures. This client, before she went into business, had been an elite athlete. Since then, she'd managed a string of "impossible" projects that would have overwhelmed most people.

She never whined or complained; she always talked about her challenges in a fact-based and nonemotional way. When I asked her how she was able to sustain such a balanced and constructive view, she answered, "Well, I use the mindset I had when I was in sports: Whenever I fail or succeed, fifty percent has to do with me and fifty percent has to do with factors beyond my control. So why kill myself if I fail or become overly carried away when I succeed? I can only focus on preparing myself and doing my best. Of course, over time I learn more about the factors beyond my control, which helps me to prepare and execute even better."

The detective mindset is also important when you face

what appear to be impossible challenges. In my work, I continuously encounter clients who face the impossible daily. In addition, I have lived through several large-scale "impossible" situations, for example the dot-com crisis in the early 2000s, the financial crash of 2008, and the COVID outbreak in 2020. To stay motivated in situations like those, you should think like a detective by recommitting to what we all know deep down inside: that nothing is impossible, and even if it is close to impossible, you can always make things better. In a way, you should be grateful for the challenges those impossible situations create because they demand that you pull the best out of yourself and others.

The detective mindset quickly turns your world into a more interesting place, one that is filled with problems to analyze. Virtually every problem can be solved. It is just a question of how much time and attention you invest.

Once you embrace that you and only you can decide how to think about yourself and the things that happen to you, you will improve your mental and physical health. By building a habit of always stepping back and deliberately deciding how to think about your challenges, you strengthen your ability to disassociate yourself from stress.

17

Always Do What Is Right for the Company

Easy to implement in your work life

Why *are you paid a salary?* Think about that question because your answer will have a major impact on how you think about yourself and how you conduct yourself at work. Before I tell you what I believe is the right answer, I want to tell you how I came up with it, because it was a turning point in my career. When I left McKinsey & Company to take on my first executive position many years ago, I was plunged into a personal and professional crisis. I was surrounded by people who seldom did what they were supposed to, often behaved in nonproductive ways, and played endless political games (since then, I have learned that this is the norm in most organizations).

I was woefully ill-equipped to lead. Everyone I'd worked with at McKinsey was extraordinarily constructive and knew how to work effectively in teams and with all types of people. The employees always, without exception, delivered according to expectations or better. Missing a deadline was unheard of; it simply never happened.

For the first six months in my new position, I struggled; I wanted to get on top of the situation and do great things, but how? I did not want to merely adopt the habits of my new company. So, I started to think deeply about my role and what my fundamental responsibility was, beyond the concrete tasks in the job description. One big question slowly started to form in my head: "Why is my employer paying me a salary?" Then the answer came to me: "I am paid a salary to think and act in the company's best interests." That was it!

Let me be clear on what I mean by focusing on the company's best interests. That is not the same thing as the best interests of your boss or the C-suite or the CEO, or any other person in the company. It is about being mindful about whether your work, achievements, and behaviors and those of the people you supervise make the company stronger, healthier, and a better place to work. If you have moral objections to the company—if you believe that its work is damaging to society, or that its management is corrupt—you should think about leaving. If not, then your job is to help the people on your team and the company to thrive.

Armed with this new perspective, I found I could think and act toward my direct reports, colleagues, and boss in ways that gave me comfort as well as clear direction. When they behaved badly, did not deliver what they were supposed to, or acted in other ways that clearly were not in the best interest of the company, I called them out. I didn't attack them; I asked them questions. If two of my direct reports did not collaborate well because of conflict, I would invite them both to my office and say something like "So, Bob and Jane, it is evident that you have some kind of conflict that impairs your work results. Can you explain to me how this situation is in the best interest of the company?"

If they tried to explain why they had this "problem" instead, I cut them off, saying, "I am not interested in why you have this problem. What I am asking you is how this situation is in the best interest of the company." Since they didn't have an answer, I told them to use the next half hour to work out a solution and report back to me. I made it clear that the problem should be fully solved and not occur again.

I found this approach to be extremely powerful. It made life so much easier, not just for me as a leader but for all the people I worked with. Suddenly, we had an understandable metric that we could use to assess our behaviors, work results, ideas, and priorities.

But that is not all the benefits. For me and the people around me, the focus on the company's best interest also made us better thinkers. Why? Because to keep our focus on the company's best interests, we had to leave our inner voices, with all their selfish demands, at home. When you bring your selfish needs to work, you inevitably leave much of your intelligence behind.

Being consciously or subconsciously governed by your selfish needs gives you tunnel vision, as you will only register the elements of your situation that relate to yourself. This bias will permeate everything you do: how you perform your tasks, how you engage with your colleagues and stakeholders, and what you will learn. Furthermore, putting your selfish needs first causes negative stress. Why? Simply because you will take everything that doesn't meet your needs as a personal affront. This means that you will most likely leave work every day feeling frustrated, angry, and unfulfilled, burdened by negative thoughts about people who, like you, allowed themselves to be governed by their selfish needs.

If you continuously build your insight into what is in the best interest of the company, you can talk to anyone with confidence, regardless of who they are or what they think. No matter how they may behave, most people understand that they should be putting their corporate responsibilities first. So long as you make it clear that that's your sole motivation, they will believe you have integrity and are not pushing your issues or opinions for your own benefit.

Another way to think about this is to ask yourself what is *always* in the best interest of the company. Here are three things:

1. Everything you do must create more value than the cost of doing it. So, regularly check the value of what you produce with those who use the results of your work.

2. Personal chemistry, different interests, appearances, or other factors should never affect the quality of your collaboration with or behavior toward others.

3. Exercise self-leadership and initiative taking: If you notice that an essential task is not being done, you are responsible at the least to find out why it's not being done by the person who is supposed to be doing it. If that person has an acceptable reason, it is not a felony if you offer to help.

Many other things are always right because they are always in the best interests of the company, but those three are a good start.

Managing a Boss Who Does Not Do the Right Thing for the Company

Yes, bosses who don't do the right thing for the company exist, and a major reason is that many companies' recruiting processes are weak or flawed. In addition, companies can be equally poor at assessing their leaders' and employees' performance. Not only do bad, incompetent, and self-serving bosses exist, they are seldom called out.

I've had my share of bad bosses. In the latter part of my executive career when I joined a company to help turn it around, the CEO seemed like a nice guy with highly developed social skills, but I quickly realized that his view of people was despicable. The most important thing for him was whether they were well-dressed and good-looking; if they didn't measure up to his standards, he wanted to fire them. An awful lot of people fell short during my time at the company. In addition, he was overly sensitive to what people outside the company thought of it. Not customers or business partners, but random people in the posh neighborhood he lived in. He would call me during weekends and order me to make radical changes in the company's operations based on some flimsy feedback from one of his neighbors. This man, my boss, represented everything I am not.

At first, I thought I should resign, but I knew I could devise and execute a plan that would make the company a much better place. So, I stayed and challenged my boss instead. Every time he wanted to fire someone or pursue some ridiculous change, I asked him to outline his thinking and specifically explain how his idea would support the best interests of the company and its turnaround. He could never explain that. Hence, he didn't fire anyone or execute his "improvement ideas." Gradually he stopped coming up with his stupid ideas, which meant that I could fully focus on our work to turn the company around, which we successfully did—despite the CEO.

What can you do if you have a bad boss? If you possibly can, my first advice to you is to leave! Few things feed our inner voices the way a bad boss does, which means constant stress and misery. But what if, for whatever reason, you can't leave? The first question to ask yourself is whether your boss's bad behavior will prevent *you* from always doing the right thing for the company. If your answer is no, you could continue doing what is right for the company and either hope that your boss will be replaced or that you will in time get noticed and rewarded for your work.

If your answer is yes, then you have two options. The first is to talk back to your boss as I did, to try to convince the boss to do the right thing (and by "the right thing" I don't mean you should try to convince the boss to quit, even if that would be the right thing for the person to do). If your boss insists that you should do as you are told, even if it is contrary to the best interest of the company (but not outright illegal), you have only one option left: to do exactly as your boss says.

What you should *not* do is to refuse or do anything else to create a visible conflict with your boss, because most people operate on the belief that "it takes two to tango" and so will assume the conflict must be partly your fault. Also, you should not complain about your boss to other people in the company, since that can backfire. You especially should not complain to your boss's boss, who most likely hired your boss and therefore has a vested interest in making him or her look good.

Sounds depressing, right? Let me give you some words of comfort. One of the surest ways to get rid of a bad boss is to do exactly what he or she says. If you make it clear to everybody that it is your boss's ideas and priorities you are acting on, and it becomes evident that those things aren't creating value, chances are that your boss will be asked to leave.

18

Write Yourself a Welcome-Back Letter

Easy to implement in your work life

Do you find it hard to get back up to speed or feel excited about work when you return from a vacation? A neat trick is to write yourself a welcome-back letter before you leave. It should contain a few words about some exciting stuff you achieved before you left, some ideas for simple but exciting tasks to pursue during your first week back, and lay out your key work priorities for the coming months

Writing this letter has several benefits. First, it allows you to relax when you are away—you won't have to worry about what to focus on when you get back or how you will get motivated, as you already have a plan. Second, it is a fun exercise, both writing the letter and then reading it after vacation.

Here's an example of one from my client Linda, the director of human resources for a global company:

Welcome back from vacation, Linda!

I hope you enjoyed your time at your brand-new summer house with your family. I assume the kids loved swimming in the lake.

You should feel energized being back at work, ready to build on all the amazing things that you achieved during the months and weeks before you went away:

- The new talent architecture was embraced by your stakeholders as a giant improvement in how the company assesses its leaders and employees.
- You managed to improve your relationship with Bob, head of services, which led to greater transparency about Services' leadership-development needs.
- You coached Jenny on leading people reviews on her own, which has increased her work satisfaction a lot as well as freed up some quality time for yourself.

What should we start with the first week back at work? Here are some ideas:

- Gather your team and ask them to share their best memories from their own vacations as well as their priorities for the next two weeks.
- Check in with Bob to discuss his vacation and what the next steps are in creating robust plans to develop his high-potential leaders.
- Outline some initial thoughts on how to improve recruiting in R&D.

Here are some of the important things you want to achieve during the next couple of months:

1. Performance Management Initiative in Global Operations—follow up with the executive team on their deadlines for the October People Review proposals.

2. By September 30, facilitate robust execution plans for all central functions in India, China, and the US.
3. By October 15, psychological safety training for all leaders in India.
4. Improve recruiting process for R&D engineers with James, head of R&D—detailed plan should be in place before November 1.

Linda, again, welcome back from vacation and to exciting times at work.

Actively Manage Your Anxiety

Moderately demanding to implement in your work life

Your inner voice is extremely anxious in its pursuit to keep you safe, which means we all get nervous and anxious. The problem is that when we do, we cannot think clearly.

A good way to reduce your overall anxiety in life is to practice mindfulness meditation daily. This will teach you how to pay attention to your breathing, which enables you to reduce your anxiety when it knocks on the door. I have been practicing mindfulness meditation for more than twenty years, and it is powerful.

However, practicing mindfulness meditation daily will not prevent you from facing situations that will make you nervous or anxious. The problem is that when we know we will soon face such a situation, we tend to deal with it in the wrong way. Either we tend to not want to think about it, because just thinking about it is painful, or we overthink it, that is, our mind inflates how bad the situation will be.

The best way to deal with these situations is to get the nervousness and anxiety out of your system before the event, so that you can look at it objectively and establish an intellectual approach.

In the sections that follow are some tools you can use to handle your anxiety. Use them as stand-alone tools or in combination, whatever works for you.

Proactively Identify All Events That Could Cause Nervousness or Anxiety

Look in your calendar and ask yourself, "Which events in the coming weeks are likely to cause me anxiety?" Print out your calendar and mark the events. Better yet, color-code the calendar, with all the challenging events highlighted in red and the rest in green.

This has many benefits. First, seeing the actual ratio between nervous-making and normal events gives you a more balanced view. The anticipation of stress can take over your mind, making you believe that your situation is worse than it is.

Second, simply marking the events is a first step toward establishing control, which in itself is a relief.

Define Your Tactics

Two to three days before a nervous-making event, sit down and think about your tactics: What are your dos and don'ts, both for your preparation and your execution? Define two or three worst-case scenarios and decide how to manage them if they happen. Revisit and refine your targets and tactics at least twice before the event. And don't forget to do a postmortem when it is over—evaluate and learn!

Public speaking is a problem for me. Though I have given hundreds of speeches, the anticipation of one still makes me sick to my stomach. Here is how I cope:

- I prepare my speeches thoroughly.
- I have a detailed plan for their first ten minutes, from the contents of my opening remarks to what my posture and body language should convey. I specifically focus on how I should relate to the audience. If there is someone in the audience I know and like, I may pretend I am talking directly to that person. Or I might zoom in on a few individuals and have some interactions with them.
- I rehearse my speech several times, experimenting with different ways of delivering it, especially its opening.

All this planning helps me to disassociate from my nervousness. No matter how stressed I am when I walk onstage, I know what I have to do each step of the way.

Write Down Your Thoughts or Talk Out Loud to Yourself

If you feel you are getting nervous the morning of the event, sit down and take out a blank sheet of paper or open your calendar to make some notes.

Write down every thought that is in your mind. Structure and logic are completely unimportant; just write and don't analyze. Then, when you have written all that you can, analyze it. If you are feeling doubtful about your presentation, debate it with yourself until you feel a sense of control over how to think.

Another method is to close your door and talk to yourself out loud. When you have gotten all your initial thoughts out and can "see" what they are, debate with yourself about whether it is logical to feel this way, and if not, ask what way would be better.

You can repeat these methods several times depending on how much time you have.

Use the 4+4 Breathing Method

If you are getting anxious just before the event, sit down and breathe in slowly for four seconds, then breathe out slowly for four seconds. Repeat this for at least two minutes. This will help bring your heartbeat and breathing back to normal, which clears your mind. You can also use this breathing method during the event if you need to.

20

Apply Logical Thinking When You Experience Uncertainty

Moderately demanding to implement in your work life

Few things set off our inner voices like uncertainty. Faced with uncertainty, we can get stressed to the point of paralysis. In high-pressure, fast-moving professional environments, things can get very uncertain indeed. Decisions are made at the top of the house that are not explained well (common), and new corporate priorities or ways of working are communicated on the intranet with no deeper explanation of why and what will happen next (equally common).

Our brain sees uncertainty as a risk, which sends the Default Mode Network into overdrive. This causes us to obsess, magnifying our sense of the risks' likelihood and magnitude.

I have worked with many clients who suffer from burnout. In virtually every case, the cause was not that they had too many things to handle, or that they worked too many hours—it was that they were holding *too many unresolved uncertainties in their minds, which they were trying to suppress instead of bringing out into the light*. The uncertainties these clients faced ranged from personal matters, such as their relationships with their spouses and their kids, to unpredictable bosses, hostile work environments, the lack of a clear vision for their professional future, and so on. Suppression of negative emotions intensifies the activities in our warning and fear centers, which create more stress.[1] Higher stress leads to hypersensitivity, which can create a self-reinforcing negative spiral, in which the subconscious's struggle with uncertainties takes up more and more mental bandwidth, making it difficult for the conscious mind to concentrate during the day and to get enough sleep at night. The more tired we are, the worse our ability to think, and the less energy and desire we have to get involved in our tasks and surroundings. We fall further and further behind.

In these situations, it is crucial that you move into action to activate another network in the brain, your executive functions. Here's a straightforward way to do this:

1. Write down those uncertainties and describe them, whether they are private or professional or both.
2. Create a simple plan for how you can work to make each a little less uncertain.
3. Do something small every day that is based on the plan or plans you have drawn up.

When doing this, ask yourself these questions:

1. What am I completely certain I should do?
2. What do I think I should do but am not certain about?
3. What am I clueless about in what I should do?

Put your answers in separate "buckets," as in the diagram below.

A logical way to address uncertainty and still be productive

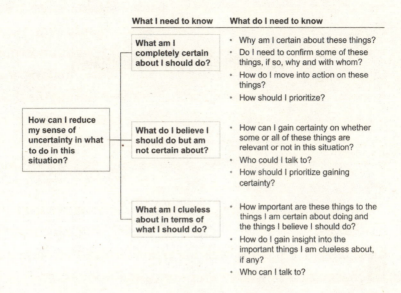

What I need to know	What do I need to know
What am I completely certain about I should do?	• Why am I certain about these things? • Do I need to confirm some of these things, if so, why and with whom? • How do I move into action on these things? • How should I prioritize?
What do I believe I should do but am not certain about?	• How can I gain certainty on whether some or all of these things are relevant or not in this situation? • Who could I talk to? • How should I prioritize gaining certainty?
What am I clueless about in terms of what I should do?	• How important are these things to the things I am certain about doing and the things I believe I should do? • How do I gain insight into the important things I am clueless about, if any? • Who can I talk to?

(How can I reduce my sense of uncertainty in what to do in this situation?)

As you do this, you will most likely see that you are quite certain about many things; this will counterbalance the Default Mode Network's storytelling relatively quickly, while reducing your stress by increasing your sense of control. It will also support the work of your subconscious, which has been aware of and struggling to resolve these uncertainties, even while you were trying to suppress them. And, most important of all, it is your first big step toward breaking the negative cycle.

21

Communicating Under Uncertainty

Moderately demanding to implement in your work life

My clients typically feel uncertain when they are put in charge of a new area and are called upon to present their plans and priorities for it.

A newly appointed CEO I worked with was facing his first board meeting. He was nervous, not only because he had been in the job for a short time, but also because he knew that two of the board members were extremely detail oriented and would demand clear answers to their questions (the previous CEO had been fired in part because he'd failed to answer their questions satisfactorily).

The worst thing you can do with detail-oriented people is to try to snow them with generalities. You must preempt their focus on details in areas where you can't supply them. A simple way to deal with this is to break down what you present into three categories, similar to those in the previous chapter:

1. The things you are completely certain about and their implications.
2. The things you believe are true but are not yet certain about and their implications.

3. The things you still do not have a clear perspective on, why it is important that you do, and what you are doing to educate yourself about them.

This is exactly what the CEO did. The result: The board was happy with the insights he had so far and respected his transparency. This allowed him to build solid relationships with them.

A logical way to communicate under uncertainty

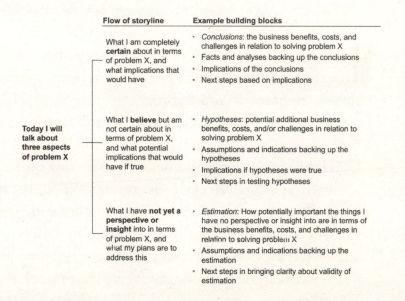

	Flow of storyline	Example building blocks
	What I am completely **certain** about in terms of problem X, and what implications that would have	• *Conclusions*: the business benefits, costs, and challenges in relation to solving problem X • Facts and analyses backing up the conclusions • Implications of the conclusions • Next steps based on implications
Today I will talk about three aspects of problem X	What I **believe** but am not certain about in terms of problem X, and what potential implications that would have if true	• *Hypotheses*: potential additional business benefits, costs, and/or challenges in relation to solving problem X • Assumptions and indications backing up the hypotheses • Implications if hypotheses were true • Next steps in testing hypotheses
	What I have **not yet a perspective or insight** into in terms of problem X, and what my plans are to address this	• *Estimation*: How potentially important the things I have no perspective or insight into are in terms of the business benefits, costs, and challenges in relation to solving problem X • Assumptions and indications backing up the estimation • Next steps in bringing clarity about validity of estimation

Always remember that to come across as knowing what you are talking about, structure is king, content is queen. In other words, the structure you use in how you talk or present is always more important than the content you put into that structure.

22

Be Smarter About Email

Moderately demanding to implement in your work life

My clients frequently complain that they're burdened by all the emails they receive. In fact, your in-box can be a highly valuable resource if you approach it analytically. Here are some simple guidelines for getting the most from your email:

1. **Measure your email volume.** Take four weeks of incoming emails and analyze them. How many messages do you receive in a typical day? Most of my clients are surprised by how few they actually get, compared with how many they feel they do. How many of the emails that you get on a typical day are specifically addressed to you? And how many require your response?

2. **Analyze who is writing the emails.** Sort your in-box by creating folders for the people who write you the most. Analyze the topics they write about and how they write. Few things are more revealing of people's mindsets, skills, and ways of thinking than how they write.

3. **Analyze which topics are inappropriate for email.** Many of the topics people write to you about via email could have been dealt with much more efficiently through other channels. Some emails request information the senders

were too ignorant or lazy to get themselves. Sometimes a quick phone chat can eliminate the need for a long, time-consuming string.

4. **Set aside thirty minutes every day to read and answer your emails.** You can of course divide it into three ten-minute sessions or two fifteen-minute sessions each day. The key is to time-box your email responses.

5. **Important: never, ever use email for emotionally sensitive topics.** And don't use it at all if you have a glitch in your relationship with the person you are sending it to. Many of my clients have made the mistake of using email to try to discuss or solve a collaboration issue; that never works and risks deepening the problem. Any type of sensitive topic is best dealt with face-to-face or, if that is not possible, via Zoom or telephone.

23

Limit Your Time on Social Media

Moderately demanding to implement in your work life

I have lost count of how many client organizations I have visited where people report they are overly stressed and have too-heavy workloads. I typically spend a few hours walking around their offices to observe and chat with employees. I focus particularly on what they have on their computer screens, which often is social media.

No wonder they are stressed! If you waste valuable work time on social media, of course you will perceive your work as demanding. In a brilliant article in *The Wall Street Journal*, Nicholas Carr summarized some interesting research on smartphones and how they interfere with our lives and our ability to perform.[1]

If you are like the typical owner of an iPhone, you'll pull it out and use it some eighty times a day, according to data Apple collects. Multiply that by 365 and you'll be using it almost thirty thousand times in a year.

What happens to your mind when you allow your smartphone to dominate your life to that extent? The research findings on that question are troubling.

Adrian Ward, assistant professor at the University of Texas at Austin, has been studying the way smartphones affect our thoughts and judgments. Using a smartphone, or even hearing one ring or vibrate, makes it much harder for us to concentrate on a difficult problem. A 2015 study showed that when people hear their phone ring but are unable to answer it, their blood pressure goes up, their pulse quickens, and their ability to solve problems declines.[2]

Ward and colleagues conducted tests to gauge participants' available cognitive capacity (how fully they can focus on a particular task), and their fluid intelligence (their ability to solve an unfamiliar problem).[3] Then he divided the subjects into three groups and tested them again. One group placed their phones in front of them on their desks, another group stowed their phones in their pockets or handbags, and a third group's phones were held in a different room.

The results were clear. On both measures, the participants with phones in another room did the best. The participants who kept their phones in their pockets or bags did worse, but not as badly as the ones whose phones were in view. In other words, your brainpower decreases as your phone's proximity increases.

It isn't just your reasoning that is impaired when phones are around. You also do worse with social skills and relationship building. In a 2013 study, participants conversed in pairs for ten minutes.[4] Half had a phone with them, half didn't. The presence of mobile phones clearly inhibited the development of interpersonal closeness and trust while diminishing empathy and understanding.

So, what to do with your smartphone? Here are three simple rules:

1. Never bring your phone into a meeting. If you're expecting an urgent call, leave the phone with a colleague who can interrupt the meeting and tell you.

2. Silence your phone and keep it out of sight when you are working on a demanding task or problem.
3. Decide on specific times during the day when you will use your smartphone.

24

Apply Logical Thinking to All Types of Problems

Demanding to implement in your work life

How can you avoid being blinded by your beliefs, experiences, and biases? By building your ability to think logically.

Thinking logically is about behaviors and habits, as well as thoughts. In particular, four habits support logical thinking:

Always use paper and pen. Our limited working memory makes it virtually impossible for us to deal with any type of problem exhaustively if all its bits and pieces are still in your head. Analyzing the problem becomes much easier when your thoughts are written down.

When you feel absolutely certain, sound a red alert. Whenever you feel completely certain about a problem and its solution, a red alert should go off in your head. Why? Because the sense of certainty can lead you to ignore signs that contradict your beliefs.

In a speech at the Oxford Union, Professor Jordan Peterson said that whenever people face a situation or a problem, they should ask themselves, "Do I need a high-resolution image of the situation, or is my default low-resolution image enough?" In my experience, most professionals act on low-resolution images of the problems they work on, leading to a lot of mistakes and misspent energy.

When I think back on mistakes I've made, they almost always occurred when I was completely sure I was right. When you have a bit of doubt, you pay much more attention to details and the gaps in your thinking.

Whenever you face a problem, you should ask yourself, "Do I know enough or need to know more about the problem to deal with it in a good way?" Or: "What am I missing that could potentially make the way I think about this problem wrong?"

List what you think you know about the problem under these three headlines:

1. The facts that indicate this is the problem.
2. The conscious or subconscious assumptions or beliefs I have that indicate that this is the problem. Ask yourself how you can validate or falsify those assumptions or beliefs.
3. The areas I don't have my head around yet. Ask yourself how you can validate or falsify information in those areas.

By focusing on the gaps and weaknesses in your view of the problem, you proactively avoid three biases:

- **The Ikea effect.** This is our tendency to place a disproportionately high value on objects that we partially assembled ourselves, including our ideas. Be aware that your inner voice will try to make you too attached to your definition of a problem and/or its solution.
- **Law of the instrument.** Your inner voice tends to make you over-reliant on familiar tools or methods, while leading you to ignore or undervalue alternative approaches. "If all you have is a hammer, everything looks like a nail." Or in a professional setting—if you work in marketing, all business

issues can be solved by marketing efforts. Remember, the problem you are facing might be an important problem, but you may not be the right person to solve it.

- **Anchoring heuristic.** As mentioned before, our inner voice tends to make us over-reliant on the first piece of information we hear, even if later additional information contradicts it.

Always, without exception, quantify a problem you face. How big is it, really? Why is it so important? Doing so helps you prioritize. If you understand the size of a problem, you can compare it to everything else on your agenda and budget your time and effort accordingly. If you understand a problem's size and the value of solving it, it is easy to calculate what you can afford to spend on it. In addition, it helps you avoid brushing uncomfortable problems under the rug. If the problem is big, you simply must address it. If it is small or nonexistent, you can treat it accordingly. I estimate that as many as 80 percent of the problems people work on in companies are either (1) nonexistent, (2) unimportant, and/or (3) addressed in the wrong way with the wrong level of resources. I base my estimate on what I have seen so far across some hundred-plus companies.

In one of the companies I worked for as an executive, we printed sweatshirts and gave them to all the leaders in the company. The motto on them read A LEADER'S BEST FRIEND: HOW BIG IS THE PROBLEM?

When you have made the list of the things you need to explore to know more about the problem, set a date and time in your calendar for when to explore them. Also, identify people or sources of data that can help you get the knowledge you need.

Don't Treat Contradictions of What You Believe to Be True as Failures or Threats

Contradictions drive progress since they spur the development of new knowledge and skills and lead to new discoveries. Even if you end up disproving that a contradiction exists, it will have led you to new insights.

Also, when you make a habit of exploring contradictions, you build your skill in identifying them. Recognizing and acting on them are core features of critical thinking.

When someone spots a gap or weakness in your thinking, don't let your inner voice make you irritated or angry. Instead, view it as a gift. It is a learning opportunity because it provides insights into both your own thought processes (in this case, that you missed something and need to address your weakness), and those of the colleague who spotted it (what thought process or analytical lens caused them to see what you didn't? Ask them!).

Start a logbook in which you continuously keep track of gaps or weaknesses your colleagues have spotted in your thinking. In time, this will become a valuable resource in honing your analytical skills.

Whenever one of your beliefs is contradicted, open your calendar and set a date and time to explore it further.

Logical Thinking as a Method— Five Exhaustive Questions to Ask

Demanding to implement in your work life

Over the years I have helped hundreds of professionals master an approach of five exhaustive questions, and without exception it has radically improved their effectiveness. The most experienced benefits are (1) an increased ability to articulate and advocate for their views, (2) faster understanding and resolution of problems, (3) improved ability to prioritize problems, and (4) more effective meetings and discussions.

Use these five logical questions when you are working with colleagues and when you are working alone; they are equally useful if you are developing solutions to your own problem or stress-testing someone else's proposals in a meeting.

1. **What is the problem I am trying to solve?** Formulate the problem as a question, making sure to include the desired outcome or outcomes.
2. **How big is the problem?** How frequently does it occur? What tangible negative consequences does it cause? What data and objective observations bear that out? What additional value and benefits can be captured by solving the problem?

3. **What are the root causes of the problem?** Which are the most and least influential? Which are the hardest and the easiest to address?

4. **Do alternative solutions exist?** If so, what criteria should we use to evaluate them? Can we learn from people who have faced and managed similar problems?

5. **What is the best solution and how can we implement it?** What are the "moment of truth" activities in the implementation? How do we break the implementation down into short-term mileposts (days, weeks, months, etc.) to assess its progress? With what frequency do we need to follow up on its progress?

In the sections that follow, I'll discuss each of these five at somewhat greater length.

Formulating the Problem

Let's say that your problem is to figure out the age of a person born in a certain year, say 1937. Most, if not all, would give the answer to the problem by subtracting from the current year and, assuming the year is 2022, answering, "The person is eighty-five years old." That is correct, but only if the person is still alive. We assumed that the person was still alive, but we didn't actually know that. If it was not the case, the whole problem and its solution changes. You must be extremely specific in formulating the problem.

A good habit is to ask questions that make you smarter about the problem up front. The following dialogue from the movie *Phenomenon,* with John Travolta, illustrates the importance of specificity:

It is important to be specific when defining a problem or a task

How old is a person born in 1937?

Is the person still alive?

↘ How old is a person born in 1937 who is still alive?

 What date was the person born?

 ↘ How old is a person born on January 31, 1937, who is still alive?

  What time was the person born?

  ↘ How old is a person born on January 31, 1937, at 11:00 a.m. who is still alive?

   Where was the person born?

   ↘ How old is a person born on January 31, 1937, at 11:00 a.m. in London and who is still alive?

    Ok, the person is ….

Striving to be specific is a key success factor in solving problems

Source: Conversation from the movie *Phenomenon*, 1996

Formulating your problem as a question that expresses what you want to achieve confers several benefits:

- Putting your goal into words forces you to go deeper into the problem, sharpening your proposed solutions.
- It creates positive energy—you are trying to make something better rather than just antiseptically solving an abstract puzzle.
- It leads naturally to the next step, which is to break the problem down into a mental fork.

Here are some sample problem formulations that are either more or less clear and specific:

Less clear and specific	More clear and specific
Improve my relationship with my colleague Robert	How can I improve the dialogue with my colleague Robert so we don't disagree so often?

Less clear and specific	More clear and specific
Reduce my monthly spending	How can I reduce my monthly spending by $500 in a sustainable way?
Spend more time with my family	How can I spend more time with my family by not working weekends and beyond office hours?
Make my boss listen to me	How can I make my boss proactively ask for my advice on topics A, B, and C?

Creating Mental Forks

Once you've formulated your problem, you need to break it down into mental forks.

A mental fork, also called an issue tree, is simply a breakdown of the problem into all of the relevant and logical aspects you need to analyze to solve it. Asking the question "What do I need to know?" is a great help in doing this.

Creating mental forks is by far the most powerful but also the most difficult trick in problem-solving. Why is that? Because its specificity is counterintuitive; it runs against the grain of how our minds normally work.

Here are examples of some simple mental forks:

Problem	What I need to know
What should I focus on?	What can I influence? What can't I influence?
How should we divide the work?	What is my responsibility? What is your responsibility?
I don't have enough time	Can my workload be decreased? Can my work process become more effective? Can I get more time? Can I increase my resources?

Here is an example of a more complicated mental fork:

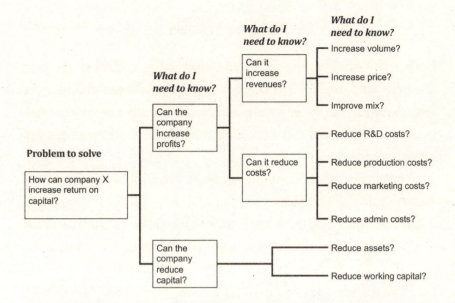

Creating mental forks is by far the most challenging part of problem-solving, but once you get the hang of it, there are multiple benefits:

1. They help you avoid common cognitive biases.
2. They help you prioritize, both when choosing among problems to address and in deciding how to solve them.
3. They are an effective way to structure your experience of the problem or similar problems.
4. They are a powerful way to translate an idea, analysis, or other task into a pragmatic execution plan.
5. They improve your memory and the amount of information you can take in and hold about a specific problem.

Mental forks are a great communication tool; they make it easier for you to guide and convince people.

Sizing the Problem

Let's say you perceive that you and your colleague Robert disagree too often. This bugs you and you want to improve the situation. So, you formulate the problem: How can I improve my dialogues with my colleague Robert, so we don't disagree so often?

The next question, which is by far the most important, is *How big is the problem?*

What you're doing here is *quantifying the value of solving the problem.* You probe this with questions like:

- How often does the problem occur? Or more specifically, how often do the two of you disagree and on what?
- What are the effects of the problem?
- What would you gain if you solved the problem, apart from avoiding the negative effects?

On a side note: I selected a problem concerning relationships in the workplace for a reason. My experience is that people tend to inflate their estimations of their work relationships, viewing them as either supergood or superbad. One thing in play here is your inner voice's cognitive bias, the "peak-end rule," in which we tend to remember the emotional high points as well as the ends of events or relationships. If two people worked together harmoniously for a long time and then suddenly had a meltdown, they will likely view their whole relationship as bad—even if the meltdown occurred after they'd spent hundreds of productive hours working together.

But let's say that your problem with Robert is real and worth addressing. You estimate that you disagree at least once a month, which leads to at least four hours of extra work for each of you as you try to come to an agreement. Furthermore, when the disagreements happen, you have a hard time concentrating on anything else for at least a couple of hours. In addition, your disagreements lead to delays in what you need to deliver to other colleagues, which causes them delays as well. Let's say three colleagues are directly affected.

All in all, you estimate that your disagreements directly cost at least three to four workdays in extra work and delays every time they occur. Since they occur once a month, the total direct costs are in the vicinity of forty workdays a year. That is the value of solving the problem, which is significant.

Root-Cause Analysis

The next question is *What are the root causes of the problem?* With Robert, the starting point is to think about when your disagreements occur and what happens when they do. What situations or subjects tend to bring them on? How do you express your disagreement? How does Robert? What does he say, and how does he show it? How do you?

You should also think about the situations that you and Robert agree about and ask the same type of questions about them. What is different in these situations—in the lead-up to the event and in the event itself?

Going through these questions, you'll find a pattern will emerge, for example:

- You and/or Robert don't prepare enough for the event (one of the most common causes of workplace disagreements) and so are not knowledgeable enough about the subject matter.
- The timing, flow, and agenda of your discussions are not effective.

- The subject matter you disagree about is more sensitive compared with matters where you agree.

Whatever combination of root causes you identify, you are now ready to solve the problem.

Solving the Problem

What is the best solution to the problem and how is it implemented? What alternative solutions are there? When you are thinking about options, it is useful to consider the following criteria. They should be phrased as questions, such as:

- **How much can a solution cost?** You want to achieve a savings equivalent to forty workdays, so that justifies a fairly high budget, provided the solution works.
- **How long may a solution take to implement?** Preferably not too long, as that can lead to a lack of focus and decreasing levels of commitment.
- **What are your capabilities?** Even if you come up with a perfect solution, it's possible you and Robert don't have the capabilities to implement it yourselves. In that case, you will need to get support, which will incur further costs in time and money.

Naturally, one option should always be "We do nothing about the problem." This is not an alternative in this case, given the huge costs of the bad relationship.

In defining the solution, you should be aware of two cognitive biases:

Bandwagon effect or groupthink. Our inner voice strongly tends to make us do (or believe) things because many other people do (or believe) them. When everyone is thinking the same, nobody is thinking much. If you think that the best solution is something that would contradict the way that people in your group habitually think, you may avoid it and select something that will go down easier. Instead of doing that, think deeply about how you can gain acceptance for the right solution.

Loss aversion. Our feelings when we lose are twice as intense as what we feel when we enjoy a gain. Your inner voice is loss averse; it would rather eliminate the risk of losing than increase the likelihood of winning. It may prompt you to avoid solutions that could incur a loss for you—a privilege, for example, or an area of responsibility or influence. Ignore those promptings and have the integrity to pursue what is correct. You will rightly feel proud of yourself.

When you have designed a solution that you both agree is optimal, ask the following questions to secure its success:

1. Who is responsible for its implementation?
2. What will you do and what will Robert?
3. Which components of the solution are easy or difficult, and how will you deal with the hard ones?
4. Will you and Robert need support from anyone else in implementing your solution, for example, your boss?
5. Will you require additional resources?
6. What are the risks and how will you manage them?
7. *What if Robert is not fully committed to the solution?* How should you manage him if that seems to be the case?
8. What metrics will you use to track the solution's effectiveness?
9. How often will you follow up on progress?
10. How well is the solution working?

Cultivate a Mindset for Inner Peace

Demanding to implement in your work life

When you have started to master your inner voice by applying the tools in this section, especially logical thinking, you are ready to fully act on this fundamental truth: *We are born incomplete and will never become complete. Hence, our driving purpose in life is to learn and develop as much as we can so that we will be a little less incomplete when we leave this world.* Many of us accept this deep down, but few of us put it into practice.

This core belief shapes virtually every aspect of how I manage myself and the people around me. If you want to let it shape your mindset, then adopt this credo:

> *It is always important to take a step back and reflect on the limitations of ideas, conclusions, and opinions. There are always new things to learn and new ways to think about old things. When events or people's disagreements put my beliefs to the test, I welcome it as an opportunity for further reflection and development.*

If you make this your core belief and let it permeate and shape your mindset, you will be able to experience the closest thing there is to what people mean when they talk about happiness: inner peace. It will also boost your integrity and focus you on ways you can grow.

Stop Having Opinions About Everything

Release yourself from the burden of constantly generating opinions about everything you experience, whether personally or via the things that other people tell you or that you read or hear in the media.

True inner peace can only be achieved when you are not completely certain that you are more right than wrong. You should understand that saying such things as "I don't know," "I don't know enough to have an opinion," or "I was wrong" are shortcuts to inner peace in a world where most people try to position themselves as knowledgeable, insightful, and right all the time, even though most of them are clueless.

Stop letting your inner voice trick you into thinking that you are knowledgeable about things you are clueless about. The most certain people I have met are invariably the ones who have no idea what they are talking about.

Resist the opportunity to talk just because you feel you have to. Stop saying things or asking questions without qualifying the relevance of them on a deeper level. Prepare meticulously for the discussions you participate in at work. Know beforehand what is relevant to ask or suggest in a meeting. Don't wing it!

Ignore your inner voice when it tries to make you believe that things you don't understand are stupid, wrong, or unnecessary. Give things you don't understand the benefit of the doubt. Not understanding something is a sign of the incompleteness we all share—and, as such, an opportunity for growth.

Cultivate a Healthy Level of Doubt

I once read a profile of the great tennis player Rafael Nadal that quoted him as saying that doubt was his key to success.[1] It sounds negative, but it makes perfect sense.

Let's say that Nadal is going to play the semifinal against Marin Cilic at Wimbledon, and Nadal has beaten him in twelve out of their fifteen matches, including the last nine. If Nadal just thinks about the statistics, he will be optimistic. But that invites overconfidence, in both his preparation for and execution of the match. So, Nadal, by cultivating a healthy level of doubt instead, keeps focused on all the necessary details, both before and during the game.

A client I've worked with for a long time has a similar attitude. I remember a conversation we had, right after he had been nominated to be a partner at McKinsey. I said to him, "Congratulations, fantastic!" He replied, "Thanks, but honestly, I think this most likely is too early. I don't think I have as solid a platform of achievements as the other colleagues who were nominated. But as I see it, the feedback from the process will be invaluable and something we can use to define clear goals to work around."

A couple of weeks later I got a call from the client. He had been elected partner.

I am by most measures a pretty good performance coach who has helped numerous professionals become happier and more successful. But I think much more about my failures than my successes. One obvious reason is that I want to become better at what I do. Another is that I am always in doubt about whether I can help my clients become more successful; the doubt helps me stay alert and present with them. But the most important reason is because it is true to the human condition—I know I am and will always be incomplete. This gives me inner peace; I am not forced to hide my development areas or shortcomings from myself and the world. Because I acknowledge them, I can address them every day.

Doubt is appropriate in any environment, but especially in the professional world. Even if you have ten good meetings with someone, there are no guarantees that the next one will be as good. Just as with a tennis match, every situation is unique and requires deliberate attention—something that is easier to establish with a healthy level of doubt. Why? Because a healthy level of doubt leads to a moderate level of anxiety! Now, anxiety is most often viewed as something bad, which it is if you suffer from too much of it. But a moderate level of anxiety is good since it keeps you sharp.

Without exception, all the people I have worked with who are exceptionally high performers, whether in business or in sports, have been "insecure overachievers" who never take anything for granted. It's served them well.

I think the attitude of embracing one's incompleteness and the importance of doubt underpins much of the hedge fund creator and management thinker Ray Dalio's thinking about radical truth and radical transparency. As he puts it:

> The greatest tragedy of mankind is that people have ideas and opinions in their heads but don't have a process for properly examining these ideas to find out what's true. That creates a world of distortions. That's relevant to what we do, and I think it's relevant to all decision-making. So, when I say I believe in radical truth and radical transparency, all I mean is we take things that ordinarily people would hide, and we put them on the table, particularly mistakes, problems, and weaknesses. We put those on the table, and we look at them together. We don't hide them.[2]

Pursue Long-Term Health Through Personal and Professional Growth

According to my friend Dr. John Arden, author of many books on the brain and health, there are five primary drivers behind good brain health, which is decisive for your overall health. They are (1) pursue a rich social life, (2) get enough sleep, (3) engage in physical exercise, (4) eat the right foods, and (5) engage in daily learning.

Working daily to make yourself a little less incomplete creates a virtuous cycle: your brain creates stronger synapses or connections, allowing you to learn and develop still more. When you are not learning, your brain senses that something is wrong and automatically refocuses you outside your comfort zone, where all development and learning takes place. As your brain's ability to learn and develop becomes stronger, it will become easier for you to identify new things to learn about and areas of yourself you need to work on, and it will be more rewarding to do so. It doesn't always have to be something big; simply performing one of your standard tasks in a new and different way will feed your brain's appetite for learning.

As you do this, your life will become more interesting, and you will become less sensitive and stressed about experiences that do not match your previous knowledge. This leads to greater adaptability, resilience, and creativity. You will become more ambitious and will dare to set increasingly demanding goals for yourself. In addition, actively learning and developing every day creates cognitive reserve, which means your brain becomes more resilient when it's damaged by accidents or disease. Your stronger brain makes you much more likely to enjoy a long and healthy life.

Pursue Respect for the Right Reasons

Our inner voice is desperate to be liked, respected, and needed. This often makes it hard for people, especially leaders, to act in the right way. If you are a leader or aspire to become one, you should cultivate a mindset that is a lot like a parent's. Whether or not they know it or admit it, the people you lead have as great a need to learn and grow as children do, and they need strong figures to set boundaries for them and model good examples (although most are less charming, creative, or well-intentioned than real kids). Like good parents, good leaders should:

- **Work toward not being needed.** Being a good leader is about making your people strong, self-sufficient, and able to shape their own destinies. If you are leading well, they will need you less and less as time passes.
- **Not hover.** Like a good parent, you should always want what is best for your people, but in many situations if you get too involved, you will stand in the way of their development. You want to avoid "the law of the instrument" or Abraham Maslow's "the law of the hammer," the cognitive bias that leads you to think that since you are a hammer, everything must be a nail. You don't have all the insights, knowledge, and experience that your people need. Actively introduce them to other people outside your team or even your organization who can help mentor them.[3]
- **Never take credit for their people's achievements, but always take some responsibility for their failures.** Whenever your people achieve something great, give them full credit and celebrate it. When they fail, ask yourself, "What should I have done differently? What did I not think of that might

have helped this person avoid failure?" Insist that you and whoever failed learn as much as possible about why the failure occurred. As noted above, *failure is inevitable. But failure without learning is never acceptable.*

- **Celebrate great behaviors and discourage bad behaviors.** Coach your people to *not* come to meetings and discussions unprepared or late, and to not complain and whine when they encounter problems.

- **Moderate their temper based on the specific situation.** Is it okay to be angry or authoritarian with the people you manage? When the situation calls for it, of course it is. I analogize the moods of a good leader to the strings on a guitar: you must use all of them. The low E string is for when you need to show your disappointment or anger or be decisive when your people are at an impasse. The high E string represents the opposite state of mind, when you are completely relaxed and hands-off and give your people total freedom to do what they do. The A, D, G, and B strings represent the gradient of moods in between.

- **Challenge and support their people.** Never stop pressing your people to stretch themselves and venture outside their comfort zones. If people constantly meet expectations or exceed them in their performance ratings, you are not stretching them enough. It should be hard for people to achieve their performance goals. At the same time, you need to support them and help them deal with whatever challenges they face. The quality of your support determines whether they like their work environment, which influences their dedication to their jobs.

- **Understand when to intervene and when to give freedom.** At times you have to manage people closely, for example, when they are new or new to what they are doing, struggling to perform, or if the stakes of what they're doing are crucial to the company's future. These simple questions can guide you: *Do your people know what they need to achieve? Do they have believable plans in place? Are they showing tangible progress as they work toward their goals?* If the answer to any of these is no, you need to step in.

If you embrace the fundamental truth that we are all incomplete, cultivate a healthy level of doubt, pursue personal and professional growth, and seek respect for the right reasons, then you are already shaping your destiny in ways you probably did not think you were capable of.

Master the Second-Biggest Obstacle for Professional Success and Well-Being: Other People

Besides managing their time, enjoying what they do, and delivering on their goals and dreams, establishing great work relationships is another area that is extremely challenging for most professionals. In nine cases out of ten, their feelings of discomfort are associated with people rather than their individual tasks and activities. The advice I give them turns on the following analogy or metaphor: *Imagine that you get to the gym and they've installed a new piece of equipment that builds a muscle group that you've never before trained. Consider the people who make you uncomfortable as a new piece of gym equipment you must master.*

Whether in the workplace or society at large, people tend to sort themselves into groups based on their perceived similarities. We simply like people whom we find similar to ourselves.

Our inner voice, which is programmed to keep us safe, is at play here. As John Bargh points out in his book *Before You Know It,* throughout our long evolutionary history, the biggest danger we faced was our fellow human beings. Excavations from ancient cities show that about one out of every three men was murdered! Being suspicious of people we don't know or who seem different from us has been a central strategy for survival for thousands and thousands of years. Discrimination is part of our biology, and for good evolutionary reasons.

In the professional world, this insecurity is revealed when we recruit or hang out with people who are the most like ourselves, rather than the people with the best qualifications and the most creativity, who are more likely to challenge our established ways of thinking. Not being able to effectively deal with all types of people makes you less competitive and relevant in the professional world, and hence weaker and less likely to survive.

In contrast, having strong, bulletproof social skills, including the ability to communicate well with and cooperate with other professionals, and if you are their boss, to lead them, confers powerful advantages for your destiny as a professional. And it allows you to love your work even more. There are virtually no barriers for what you can achieve if you can deal with any type of person.

Furthermore, cultivating a healthy social life is key for your short- and long-term performance, development, and health. Actively maintaining a personal *and* professional life across several social contexts where people are different from you forces you to continuously develop the brain areas devoted to social skills and empathy. You should nurture and maintain healthy, reciprocal relationships at work by helping people and by forming buddy relationships for support and inspiration. Regularly spending time with people who respect and love you for who you are and not based on how well you perform—for example, your family and friends—makes you less prone to dwell negatively on your failures and thus more resilient.

A good and diverse private and professional social life (1) increases the level of oxytocin (the love hormone) in you, (2) grows your mirror neurons (neurons hosting social skills), (3) develops your problem-solving skills, and (4) improves your attention and ability to focus. Furthermore, it decreases your cortisol levels (stress hormones) and calms your nervous system's activities. Since we are highly social creatures that have thrived through our capacity to communicate, when we are deprived of healthy, reciprocal relationships, our risk of health problems is heightened.

Cultivate and Pursue Priorities Outside Work

The clients I work with who seem to have the most relaxed view of their work demands are the ones who actively maintain and pursue other priorities that are just as strong, whether they are family, friends, or hobbies. Note: I am not talking about clients who only *say* they have other priorities (which most do), but clients who actively pursue them.

Does this give them a better work-life balance? Yes, for sure. But an even more profound benefit is that they accelerate their skills and self-awareness, becoming more effective across all of their priorities. Why is that? Because the need to balance forces them to become smarter about how they pursue each priority.

I see this with the junior elite hockey players I coach. They also have dual priorities: become world-class hockey players while succeeding at school. I don't have statistics, but I have seen many of them outperform elite hockey players who are not in school and can focus on the sport full-time. I think the logic is simple: if you can't devote your whole life to hockey, you need to be extremely deliberate in your practice and performance goals, so that the time you do spend on hockey yields the maximum return.

If you have a family, set goals together and constantly

evaluate what is and isn't working. Take an active interest in your spouse's life and share and ask for advice on the challenges you face at work.

If you are struggling to create a healthy balance between your work and other priorities, use the method described in chapter 6, "Create a Time Budget and Track Your Time Every Day." This method, together with your own version of daily journaling and actively time-boxing some of your work activities, will allow you to achieve an optimal balance.

Cultivate and Pursue Priorities at Work

Few things bring us better mental health than feeling we are part of a warm and helpful community. You can do three things to help build community at work:

Be a giver. Help someone who is struggling. When you help someone, you take a pause from your own worries, which relaxes you. And when you succeed in helping someone, you get energizing feedback telling you that you are okay, strong, and have control.

Helping someone also brings health. Research indicates that people who suffer from serious illnesses, such as cancer, have better recovery rates if they help others; it gives them a release from their own anxieties, which likely strengthens their immune systems.

But exercise caution. Helping others can exhaust you as well as take focus from your own goals and aspirations, so create a budget for how much time you spend on it. Research indicates that one hundred hours per year is the magic number, which amounts to a couple of hours a week.[1]

Build a network of buddies. My sense is that peer apprenticeship is weak in most organizations. So, my recommendation is that you develop and maintain a network of buddies to share your goals, aspirations, challenges, and good practices with.

A peer network can play many different roles; one of the most important is to make the workplace feel warmer. One good idea is to team up with a peer or buddy around your individual goals and aspirations and then spend thirty minutes or so together weekly or biweekly to discuss each other's progress and setbacks.

As a professional and executive, my first line of support was always my peers. It should be yours, too. Make it happen!

Define ground rules with the people you work with. Not knowing how to relate to team members causes unnecessary stress and uncertainty, as well as unwanted surprises, such as misunderstandings, conflicts, and undesirable team behaviors. My recommendation is to spend time together thinking through the ground rules you and your colleagues should aspire to uphold to work effectively together. Then, follow up on them frequently.

Here are the ground rules that one of my clients developed with his team:

- Don't be a jerk.
- Work hard, play hard.
- No one is perfect, and people learn best by stepping outside their comfort zone and making mistakes.
- Don't make excuses. When you make a mistake, own it and learn from it.
- Strive to do everything to the best of your abilities the first time—then do it better the next time.
- Be brutally honest with one another. Grow thick skin.
- Keep each other informed—overcommunicate. Bad news is not like wine, it doesn't get better with age.

What you should avoid at work:

- Persistent and perpetually negative people, who will exhaust you.
- Passive-aggressive people, or people who pretend to care about you but spend most of their time telling you about their latest petty problems and inviting you to feel sorry for them.
- Hanging solely with people who are similar to yourself or have similar beliefs and backgrounds. These relationships dull rather than sharpen your brain. As your levels of stress hormones rise, your altered neurochemistry impairs your brain's circuitry.

In this section I offer you multiple proven tools and principles to build your social skills, including how to develop, interact with, and communicate with all types of people, establish yourself as a trusted adviser to peers and senior executives, get your ideas accepted, lead change, and hire the right people.

Develop Aspirations for How You Want to Be Perceived

Easy to implement in your work life

The sole purpose of your work is to bring value and benefits to others. Your own needs are always secondary. By excelling at delivering value and benefits to others, you will expand and develop your capabilities and advance in your job. But it's not enough to simply be a productive colleague—you must be *perceived* as such. To do that, it helps to make your aspirations public and explicit.

Build a Two-Page Aspirations Document That Answers Three Key Questions

To fully leverage the power of your aspirations, you must invest time and effort in formulating them. To start, you need to write them down. Writing them down makes them real—this is the first step to getting them "into your system."

The end product of your work will be a two-page document outlining how you want to be perceived. This document will serve as your starting point, but you can adjust and update it as you develop and refine your aspirations and your capabilities. Don't be shy! Dare to set your aspirations high.

Don't just aspire to be thought of as reliable—aspire to be thought of as C-suite material. Don't just aspire to be trusted; aspire to be respected and admired.

The first step in creating this document is to answer three questions in writing (see table below).

1. **How would people describe you?** How would you like your colleagues, boss, and other stakeholders to think of you? More specifically, what two or three distinguishing attributes would you like these constituents to state when asked about you? Their answers should be the things that would make others want to meet you, work with you, or hire you. Be specific. Rather than "He is a good person," write statements like:
   - He can solve complex problems.
   - She knows the strengths and development needs of the people she works with and effectively expands their capabilities.
   - I feel confident that I could put this person in any type of position given her commitment, analytical skills, and ability to mobilize people around what is important.

   The more detailed your answers, the easier it is for you to regulate and shape your behaviors and approaches to achieve the desired perception.

2. **What feedback would you want people to give you spontaneously?** What impression do you leave on people when you engage with them, whether informally, in meetings, or via email? Ask yourself, "What would I want my colleagues, my boss, and my other stakeholders to think about me after we have interacted?" Think of attributes that would make people seek you out as a problem-solver

or diplomat, or someone who always goes the extra mile. The idea is to create an ever-present mental framework for your interactions with people. Focus on specific and concrete feedback on both your preparation and your execution. Here are some examples of the types of responses I might aspire to: "Stefan, your help on this matter has truly been invaluable, now I know exactly how to manage this" or "Stefan, it is uncanny how well you understand my strengths and development needs and how you help me expand my abilities."

3. **What role models do I have?** Identify specific people you know who model the skills and behaviors you would like people to attribute to you—and I used the plural deliberately, since one person is unlikely to display all of the behaviors and skills you aspire to. The benefit of this is that you can not only study them but talk to them about how they go about creating the impact you hope to have. Remember the habits and attitudes of intrinsically motivated professionals: "The most effective way to learn a new task is to copy how another person is performing the task. When I face a new task, I observe and talk to someone who knows how to perform the task." Perhaps one of your role models would like to be your coach. If you don't ask, you'll never know.

Table: Elements of an Aspirations Document

Element	How people describe you	Feedback that people volunteer	My role models
Detailed question	What specific attributes would people ascribe to you?	What would people say to me after we interact?	How do they do the things I want to be able to do?

Element	How people describe you	Feedback that people volunteer	My role models
Example answers	He can solve complex problems. He applies analytical skills to mobilize staff.	With your help, now I know how to manage this. You really understand my development needs.	I admire Bill for his executive presence, and Pam for her ability to always get her ideas accepted and implemented.
Benefits	Helps you shape your behaviors to change perception.	Creates framework for how you prepare and interact with people.	By learning from someone how to master what you want to master, you will radically speed up your development.

One of my clients, Terry, a senior adviser at a global tech advisory firm, uses her written aspirations in a practical way: every day she plans, executes, and evaluates at least two interactions based on how she wants to be perceived.

Here is how she wants people to perceive her professional impact:

What I Would Like My Stakeholders to Say When Asked About My Professional Impact

My clients:

- Terry has a unique ability to help us understand and discuss our most pressing issues in a clear and to-the-point manner.
- She brings positive energy, which energizes us.
- We get the best possible result when we engage with Terry. She has the ability to understand our unique context and needs.

My colleagues:

- We see Terry as an up-and-coming leader who will contribute greatly to our firm's future growth.
- Terry is a high-performing yet humble professional.
- Terry has the ability to interact with and inspire all types of colleagues, regardless of their background, age, or experience.

What Feedback I Would Like My Stakeholders to Give Me

My clients:

- You have made me see the issues at hand from a new perspective. The way you led us through this problem-solving exercise was excellent. We grew as a leadership team, even though we have worked together for years.

My colleagues:

- When working on your team, you trigger me to excel and grow in ways I did not believe possible. My achievements when working with you are a surprise even to me—am I really this good?
- As your leader, Terry, I feel I need to shape up my leadership skills to keep up with you.

My role models:

- *Executive presence*—Barbara has a style of presenting and shaping her message that draws people in. When she is onstage, the audience is fully immersed and hangs on her every word. This is inspirational.

- *Community building*—Robert sees the value of bringing our team together. He creates a learning and sharing environment.
- *Conflict resolution*—Kim knows how to work through sensitive situations with senior leaders. I wish I could be as good as he is in facilitating discussions for large groups of people.
- *People leadership*—My husband, Jim, coaches me, our kids, and our friends in a reflective and thoughtful way.

Here's how Terry has experienced the benefits of defining and sharing her aspirations:

My aspirations are very personal, and I have only shared them with a small selection of key leaders at my firm. I have experienced many positive effects from doing so. Besides making it much easier for me to prioritize in certain situations based on what is most important to me, it's strengthened the sponsorship and attention I receive from those leaders, who proactively offer me advice on how to progress and grow.

If You Are a Leader, Involve Your Colleagues and Staff in Developing and Following Up on Your Aspirations

Once you have produced a complete first draft of your aspirations document, you should collect feedback on your leadership. You can easily do this by surveying your current staff, three to five people who formerly reported to you, your current peers, and three to five of your former peers. You can do the survey in a Word document or, if you have access to a digital survey tool, you can use that. The answers must be anonymous because you don't want to be swayed by a particular person's answer; that is, knowing who the person is could affect how you analyze the answer.

You should look for common themes. People tend to be constructive even when they are anonymous, especially as your feedback survey shouldn't include any rating questions, only questions that ask for descriptions of how they experience your leadership.

You can add questions if you want to ask about other things, but make sure you include these questions:

1. How would you describe my strong sides as a leader and coach, as regards my behaviors and skills?
2. Please provide a few concrete examples of how these strengths show themselves in my performance.
3. How would you describe my most important needs for development—the areas where I could improve?
4. Please provide a few concrete examples of how these needs for development show themselves in my performance.
5. Do I have any habits or behaviors that you believe I need to tone down or stop to be a more effective leader?
6. Please provide a few examples of how these habits and behaviors negatively impact my effectiveness as a leader.

Doing one of these feedback surveys has many benefits. First, the answers provide you with amazing insight into how people perceive your leadership. Second, you will get many useful ideas about which areas you need to develop. And finally, you send a strong signal that you are committed to your development as a leader.

Complete Your Aspirations Document

Once you have compiled and read through the feedback you got from the survey, use it to refine your answers to the four questions, including thinking of and formulating several leadership behaviors you should strive for. When you feel that your aspirations document is finished, read through it several times to make sure it is relevant, important, and inspiring. You can also share this first complete version with a handful of people who are close to you and whom you trust, such as family members, friends, and fellow leaders.

Involve Your Staff in Monthly Follow-Up Meetings

When you have a first complete version of your dream document, it's time to involve your staff. Share the document with them and make them a force that helps you on the journey toward your aspirations.

Most leaders find it difficult and unpleasant to open up to their colleagues and staff. If you are one of them, you'll just have to tough it out, because doing things this way is incredibly potent and effective. First, it's cleverer and much better to own your weaknesses than try to hide them, as your staff can see them much better than you can.

Second, you make your staff aware of what you're striving for. This will change their expectations and deepen their understanding of you as a leader. It will also make them more inclined to help you on your journey. If you have a problem such as losing your temper when you get stressed and you acknowledge it in your dream document, it will make your staff more tolerant when you do blow your top because they know this is a problem that you are working on.

Third, by sharing your leadership dream with your staff,

you put pressure on yourself to be serious about your work on yourself. Telling others what you intend to do is a fantastic way to make yourself deal with what you've said you're going to do.

Fourth, when you open up as a leader and involve your staff in your development, you send the strongest signal you can that development is vital to you and to them.

Send Out Your Aspirations Document and Call for a Meeting

Send your aspirations document to your staff and call them to a meeting to go through and discuss the document.

The agenda for the first meeting is simple. Start by thanking everyone for their feedback, then go through the document. It is important that you openly go through any "negative" feedback from the staff. If you don't do this, your staff will not regard you as honest and serious, which means that they won't be honest and helpful during this or any follow-up meetings.

After you've gone through your aspirations, let your staff provide their individual reflections and ideas. Ask if they think anything is ambiguous or unclear.

Conclude the meeting by setting the date for the first monthly follow-up meeting to discuss your progress. Then summarize the discussion and write down the most important insights. Add your notes to your document as an appendix. This will be like a journal for you.

Run the monthly follow-up meetings in a similar way, but it may be a good idea to let the staff begin these meetings by sharing their observations on how your development journey is going. Ask them for concrete examples of what is working well or less well.

Afterward, you can then give your own self-assessment. These meetings probably don't need to be any longer than an hour. Continue them for a year.

Some leaders I've worked with have made these monthly meetings a permanent part of their development; they've also become a forum for colleagues or staff to discuss their own ambitions and development. Discussing development has become a natural part of everyday life for these leaders and their colleagues and staff—a part of their culture.

Make a Habit of Asking for Feedback

Easy to implement in your work life

I push most of my clients to ask for feedback all the time. Why? Because the people you ask for feedback from will feel respected, important, and influential. Beyond that, they will give you:

- Useful ideas for how you can improve.
- Insights into how the people around you think and work.
- Less resistance in the future, thanks to their increased sense of ownership and importance.
- A more deliberate mindset for how you orchestrate your interactions and dialogues (since you know you will be asking for and receiving feedback).

How do you do this regularly? Commit yourself to always ask for feedback after any interaction—for example, after meetings, interviews, requests for input, any type of delivery, quick calls, and email exchanges.

Here are some examples of feedback questions:

- Was this helpful for you?
- Was this what you expected?
- Was this time well invested for you?

- What can I do in the future to help you and add value in similar situations?

If you don't regularly meet the people who depend on your work, you should reach out to them at least twice a year for feedback. Depending on how many there are, you could do this in person or via a simple survey. Ask them:

- How well does my work support your performance?
- Do any specific aspects of my work serve you really well?
- Are there any specific aspects of my work that I can improve? If so, how?

29

Make It Easy for People to Follow Your Advice and to View You as a Thought Leader

Easy to implement in your work life

An important aspect in shaping your destiny as a professional is to deliberately work to be viewed as a great thought leader and adviser, whether by peers or senior leaders and executives. You'll know you have achieved this status when you are regularly asked to share your feedback, experience, or insights on topics people are working on (or should be working on). To achieve this status, you must master the tools around logical thinking in Section Two of this book.

Although peers and senior leaders are all human beings who share many similarities in how they approach their jobs and how they process information, you need to approach them in somewhat different ways to be viewed as a trusted adviser or thought leader.

Play Down Your Own Importance

Giving well-intentioned solicited or unsolicited advice to peers is often far riskier and more complicated than it should be. This is very much the case when the peers are all males, who tend to be absurdly territorial in their areas of responsibility. What makes this even more absurd is that the more clueless they are about solving problems in their areas of responsibility, the more territorial they become and the less help they seek (no wonder companies end up in trouble).

Often when leaders are struggling, their boss calls for external help from colleagues who could have relevant insights. If you get such an invitation, you need to be very deliberate in how you behave toward these leaders.

My friend and mentor John Douglas created and managed the FBI's criminal profiling program; he is extremely astute in analyzing the motives behind people's actions, not least those of serial killers. Local police departments often call on him for advice when they are contending with a series of unsolved violent crimes. The officers are generally skeptical when he arrives, particularly the older and more experienced ones. John handles them not just well, but in a completely world-class way.

When all the police who have worked with the unsolved crimes have gathered, he opens with, "First of all, I'd like to say that, from my own experience, it is far from certain that I can add anything to your work. If I am going to be able to give you any suggestions and advice at all, I need to know about your insights and work so far. But I'd once again like to emphasize that I am far from sure that I can add anything of value beyond what you have already done."

In talking down his status, John deflects the implication that the group lacks competence, defusing the threat he represents to its current structure, identity, and internal relations. Lowering your status makes you less threatening and easier to accept. It also forces John himself to remember to be humble and open-minded, to be a better listener.

Then, the police take him through their work. They review all the unsolved crimes, the investigations they have done, the insights they have gotten. It takes a long time, but John listens patiently and takes notes.

By listening to others and respecting their previous work, he raises their status, which makes them feel important. He also lets them guide him into the work, which creates security, because he hasn't simply commandeered their work product, which they spent hours and days and weeks compiling and analyzing. That he lets them talk about their work in their own way gives them a sense of autonomy and ownership of the process.

Once he has reviewed everything, John says, "Yes, it's as I thought, you have done everything possible that you could and should have done in this situation." He summarizes what he has been told thus far, showing them that he has listened, and bolstering their status by acknowledging how good a job they have done thus far.

After his recap, he continues, "It is just as I said in the beginning, I'm unsure whether I can add anything here. The only thing I can think of, and I'm not sure it adds anything, is perhaps to take a closer look at this aspect, or perhaps that one. . . ."

His restating and confirming his initial uncertainty about what he can contribute, but also carefully suggesting one or two small potential actions, leads to several fantastic things. The police now feel that John is part of their group; they can relate to him, which makes them receptive to his suggestions. And by keeping the number of suggestions low, he makes it much easier for them to act.

John's methods can work for any outside consultant who comes into a new, change-averse, defensive environment and wants to create good conditions for cooperation. (1) You tone down your own status and raise that of others or at least meet them on the same level. (2) You tread carefully by listening and allowing your clients to drive the process, so they feel secure in their roles and their autonomy. (3) You behave non-threateningly, to make it easier for the group to accept you as a new member and relate to you. (4) You communicate that you want to help and be part of the team and not take the glory for the group's work, which is perceived as fair and makes it easier for you to get into and gain influence in new contexts. (5) You present a limited amount of advice or potential actions, lowering the threshold for acceptance because it is perceived as eminently manageable.

John's method works. I know it because I have adopted it myself. Use it and I can guarantee that peers and colleagues will not just trust you, but actively seek you out for advice.

Handle Peers with Oversimplified Beliefs Carefully

People with oversimplified beliefs are particularly tough to deal with.

It is much easier to debate different views with people who are thoughtful, knowledgeable, and capable of forming a more complex picture of the cause behind a problem. Such people realize they do not know everything and welcome dialogue with others with different ideas. They regard good-faith challenges to their ideas as opportunities to learn something new.

On the other hand, people who are completely committed to an oversimplified understanding of the cause of a problem are almost impossible to convince otherwise—at least in the short term. This combination of low information and high confidence is known as the Dunning-Kruger effect.[1]

Why is it so hard to convince such people? Because (1) the more vehemently they deny your point, the more vehemently you argue for it, making the situation more fraught; and (2) the questions you ask are too probing. Because these people have neither good answers nor good counterarguments, they take such questions personally and respond defensively. Their thinking shuts off while their emotional center lights up, which means they become even more irrational.

Research shows that people who feel that they are being challenged not only shut down their thinking but adhere more fervently to their beliefs. Why is that? Because being challenged makes them feel bad! *Especially* when they have no good answers.

Display Genuine Curiosity to Follow the "Liar" to the Door

So, what to do? Just recently I worked with a client who had to convince her peers to accept and implement a new way to manage risk in their respective departments. The response my client got repeatedly was "We have tried this before and it does not work, nor did it bring any value to the department." Based on my experience as both a coach and an executive, in ninety-nine out of a hundred situations, this is just a knee-jerk reaction from people who want to get someone off their backs.

I told my client that whatever she does, she should not continue to argue her point. Instead, in a nonthreatening way, she should ask questions and display genuine curiosity about her colleagues' claim that they have "tried it before but it did not work nor bring any value." I call this approach "follow the liar to the door."

I prepared a list of potential questions for my client to ask, for example:

"How interesting you have tried this before. Please let me know more because your insights could help me become smarter about how to do this myself."

"Tell me more about when you tried this, what was the goal?"

"How did you go about trying this? In what steps did you do it?"

"What challenges did you experience, and how did you manage them?"

"What would you do differently today if you tried it again?"

In answering my client's questions, her peers will reveal their actual knowledge and experience. If they have indeed tried what she suggested, now she has the detailed proof and can scrap her proposal. If not, the questions will help her reposition her proposal so that it reduces their resistance. At the same time, she is showing genuine interest in them and their experiences, which makes them that much more likely to listen to her and what she suggests.

How did it go? My client managed to get her peers' commitment. The new way of managing risk has been implemented in all their departments.

Becoming a Thought Leader and Adviser to Senior Leaders and Executives

One universal challenge for most professionals is to gain attention from senior leaders. Here's a practical step-by-step approach you can use.

First, senior executives can never get too many insights or gain too much knowledge about topics directly or indirectly influencing their business today and in the future. The more insight and knowledge, the better decisions and choices senior executives are likely to make. Whatever you bring them needs to be viewed as something helpful that can potentially make them more successful. Therefore, *always quantify the value of the insights or knowledge you share*—this makes the executives interested as well as helps them to prioritize among all the issues they face. If your insight yields bigger potential value compared to some of the other things they are spending their time on, chances are good it will be considered. If not, what you bring will only be regarded as noise or at best interesting.

Let's say that your work generates knowledge or insights you think should be further explored by some senior executives at your company. Here's what you should do.

Identify the senior executives who you think would benefit from it. Read whatever you can get hold of about the leaders, their backgrounds, and areas of responsibility. Pay special attention to any statements made by the leaders about their ambitions within their areas of responsibility—what do the senior leaders want to achieve and why?

Here are some examples of relevant research you can pursue:

What	For example
The senior executive's experience and professional journey.	Check LinkedIn. If the senior executive joined your company within the last 12–24 months, skim the annual reports from the company where the senior executive worked before. Do a media search to see what, if anything, has been written about the senior executive. Talk with 3–5 people who have any type of exposure to the senior executive—people both in and outside your company.
The senior executive's journey and ambitions at your company.	Study your company's annual reports and what is written about the senior executive and his or her areas of responsibility. Get hold of any material that describes the plans and strategies for the senior executive's area of responsibility.

As a senior executive I am not interested in wasting my time listening to insights or knowledge on an overall or general level; I am interested in believable and actionable insights that can—at least theoretically—generate real and measurable business value: dollars and cents. Nor am I interested in listening to advice from people who have not thoroughly considered their insights' feasibility. Furthermore, I want to feel that I am seen and understood, and that what is brought to the table is specifically relevant for my situation, which shows me that people are dedicated and have put real effort behind what they want me to focus my limited attention span on.

If you have several insights, compare them by using this simple framework:

Estimation of the business value and effort required per insight you potentially could bring to the senior executive

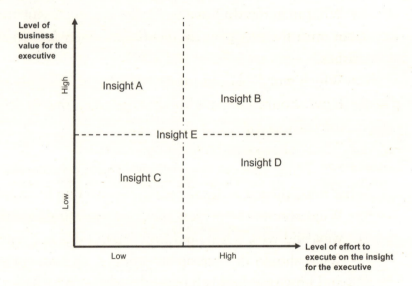

When you have made your choice of the insight to bring forward, what steps should you take to make the executive more likely to act on it?

a. Further analysis to qualify it? If so, how? In what steps?
b. Immediately improving decision-making and/or prioritization? If so, how and in what topics or situations?

Next question is to build your story around the insight.

A simple but powerful way to build skills in effective communication is to use the Know, Think/Feel, and Do model. View it as a powerful mental fork you can use for any type of communication situation.

Prepare for its use by answering the following questions:

1. **What must the executive know when the meeting finishes?**
   - How do I formulate this knowledge in the clearest way?
   - What does the executive currently know?
   - How long must the meeting be for the executive to absorb this knowledge?
   - What material do I need as support?
2. **What must the executive think and feel when the meeting finishes?**
   - Which words should I use?
   - How should I behave (body language, tone of voice, intensity, etc.)?
   - Where should we have the meeting?
   - What time of day?
3. **What must the executive do when the meeting finishes?**
   - What should the person continue to do but in a new way, and why, when, and how should this happen?
   - What should the person stop doing, and why, when, and how should this happen?
   - What should the person start doing, and why, when, and how should this happen?

Answering these simple questions increases your chances of acting wisely and with insight, which builds your ability to act with a sense of authority. They're also excellent preparation for large meetings.

As mentioned, this model for planning and executing your communication works well on all types of topics and situations:

The know-feel-do framework for effective influencing and communication

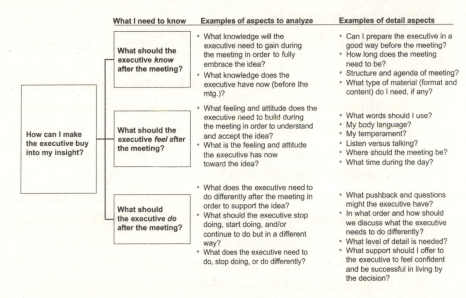

	What I need to know	Examples of aspects to analyze	Examples of detail aspects
How can I make the executive buy into my insight?	What should the executive *know* after the meeting?	• What knowledge will the executive need to gain during the meeting in order to fully embrace the idea? • What knowledge does the executive have now (before the mtg.)?	• Can I prepare the executive in a good way before the meeting? • How long does the meeting need to be? • Structure and agenda of meeting? • What type of material (format and content) do I need, if any?
	What should the executive *feel* after the meeting?	• What feeling and attitude does the executive need to build during the meeting in order to understand and accept the idea? • What is the feeling and attitude the executive has now toward the idea?	• What words should I use? • My body language? • My temperament? • Listen versus talking? • Where should the meeting be? • What time during the day?
	What should the executive *do* after the meeting?	• What does the executive need to do differently after the meeting in order to support the idea? • What should the executive stop doing, start doing, and/or continue to do but in a different way? • What does the executive need to do, stop doing, or do differently?	• What pushback and questions might the executive have? • In what order and how should we discuss what the executive needs to do differently? • What level of detail is needed? • What support should I offer to the executive to feel confident and be successful in living by the decision?

The next step is to think through the best way to deliver your insight to the senior executive. What would be the best approach? Is it trying to get a one-on-one meeting? Or is it getting yourself on the agenda to make a brief presentation in a bigger setting where the senior executive takes part? Could you get the insight in front of the senior executive through influencers, for example, your boss, people reporting to the senior executive, others?

Based on what you know about the senior executive through your research, it will not be hard to figure out what the best and most likely way will be to connect with the executive.

With senior executives truly dedicated to their work and to do good by the company, it can often be just as simple as sending them an email with your insight attached. These types of executives are likely to explore what you sent them and, if relevant, call you to a meeting to learn more from you.

If you get a meeting to discuss your insight with the senior executive, you need to secure your executive presence or gravitas: you need to command your topic but stay calm, act with integrity, and display genuine curiosity about the world of the senior executive.

This means three things:

1. *Talk about your insight with integrity.* Discuss it using the same structure for when you deal with uncertainty; that is, (1) what you are certain about that makes it relevant for the executive, (2) what you believe but are not certain about that makes it relevant for the executive, and (3) what you do not yet have a view about whether it is relevant for the executive. This way of talking gives you credibility as a mindful thinker and also invites dialogue for the executive to share perspectives.

2. *Always have the end in mind when you prepare and engage in a dialogue with an executive.* If the executive asks you what the immediate implications are if your insight is relevant, you should be able to share a perspective on that. One practical way to do that is to break the implications down by thoroughly working through the Do part of the Know, Think/Feel, and Do model for communication. If the insight is relevant for the executive to act upon, what should the executive immediately stop doing (for example, pause a decision), start doing (engage with the executive's boss or board on the insight you have brought), and/or continue doing but in a different way (add your insight as an additional aspect of how the executive normally engages with certain stakeholders, for example, customers)?

3. *Make it real and personal.* Get to know the executives' fears and desires in their jobs and in relation to the insight you are discussing. Executives are human beings just like

yourself; they are more emotional than rational. They, like most people, tend to work harder to avoid what they are afraid of than to pursue what they desire. To probe this, ask questions like these:

- What is your experience with similar insights like this? What was the context? What worked well, what worked less well, why?
- What parts of your organization would be affected the most by this insight? What is their experience with similar insights? Are there any aspects of this insight that would be hard for them to accept or understand? Why? How would you think about overcoming those challenges? What would be easy? What would be difficult?
- What about your team and the people who report to you? Who would be most affected by this insight? What is their experience with similar insights? Are there any aspects of this insight that would be hard for them to accept or understand? Why? How would you think about overcoming those challenges? What would be easy? What would be difficult?
- If you think about yourself, your overall time commitment, and other priorities, are there any aspects of this insight that would be challenging for you to execute? Why? How would you think about overcoming those challenges? What would be easy? What would be difficult? Is there anything I could do to help?

If you use the steps I have described, you are well positioned to be viewed as a mindful thought leader and adviser. Chances are that you will be called upon by the executive on many other topics and situations going forward, whether or not the executive acted on the insight you brought in on this specific occasion.

30

Don't Avoid Difficult People, Embrace Them

Easy to implement in your work life

A common theme in my work with clients is their complaints about the people they can't relate to and don't want to work with. I understand why. When we face people we perceive as being "difficult" to work with and relate to, our natural tendency is to shy away and, if possible, change contexts. Hence, few things can demotivate us as much as when we need to engage in interactions or meetings with difficult people.

But the world is filled with "difficult" people. So, if you want to grow and shape your destiny, you must master the art of transforming difficult situations with difficult people into productive ones.

There are two types of difficult people. The first I call *truly difficult people*. These people have low energy, are inward looking, display negative attitudes toward everything, are incapable of focusing on anything except what is impossible, and are fundamentally unable to adopt a more positive outlook on themselves and their contexts. Here my principle is simple: life is too short to deal with these types of people.

The other type of difficult people are *insecure people*. Given their insecurity, they can be difficult to deal with since they are extremely risk averse and unproductive. They see risks everywhere. Some of them can also be downright nasty or display abusive behaviors. But insecure people should not demotivate you. On the contrary, they can fuel your motivation to help them. Reducing their insecurity can be the key to unlocking their potential and increasing their well-being.

To help an insecure person excites me, especially when I see the person start to take charge and shape his or her own destiny by focusing on the unlimited opportunities that our personal and professional lives offer.

When you face what you believe is a difficult person, step one is to activate your detective mindset. Take your feelings and needs out of the equation. Think about the person the way you think of unfamiliar gym equipment. Once you've mastered it, it will be of great service to you. Another useful approach when dealing with a difficult person, someone I instinctively dislike or find it hard to establish a productive dialogue with, is to remind myself that the person is someone's child. Using this perspective, I then ask myself if I would like someone to have similar thoughts about my own son, Ramses. Of course not! This approach not only helps me disassociate myself from my negativity; it enables my sympathy to kick in.

Once you have disassociated your emotions from the person and the situation, use the problem-solving techniques I told you about in the section "Shape Your Destiny: Evolve Your Mindset to Become the Superstar You Can Be."

Be deliberate in how you plan and execute your interactions with these people going forward and try to learn from them. For this, you can use the Daily Goals method I previously described: define a desired outcome, devise tactics to achieve it, evaluate the extent to which they worked, and then repeat them, focusing on what you need to change as a result of your evaluation.

I've had clients who completely changed their attitudes toward people they did not want to work with after using this approach for just two weeks. Most tell me that it helped them improve relationships in other parts of their lives as well.

Here are some additional techniques you can use. Make sure you include them in your tactics when you define your daily goal of dealing with someone difficult.

Have Difficult or Challenging Meetings Walking Outside

If you have a challenging meeting with an insecure or otherwise difficult person coming up, it might be a good idea to meet outdoors. Why? So you have an excuse to avoid eye contact!

It can be more difficult to process your thoughts when you are talking to someone face-to-face. That's because you tend to look at their facial expressions to gauge their reactions. Because your mind is trying to carry out two processes at the same time, you think more slowly, which is not good if the conversation is challenging.

So, think about walking side by side instead. You will most likely think better. And if not, at least you'll get some fresh air and exercise.

Walking and talking isn't the only trick you can take advantage of. Here are four others. The last three come from the extraordinary book *Before You Know It: The Unconscious Reasons We Do What We Do,* by the social and cognitive psychologist John Bargh.[1]

Have Your Meeting After Sundown

I picked up this trick many years ago from the late Peter Jonsson, the world-renowned psychotraumatologist and crisis-management expert. The underlying logic is that human beings have poor night vision, which subconsciously makes us feel vulnerable when it is dark. When we feel vulnerable, one of our key strategies to reduce our sense of vulnerability is to be close to other people. So, chances are that if it is dark, the person you are meeting with will be less inclined to be critical and oppositional, and more focused on contributing to a good and productive atmosphere.

Give the Person Something Hot to Drink

Physical warmth or coldness affects whether we experience social warmth or coldness. Experiments show that people who held a hot cup of coffee—even for a few seconds—and then read a description of a person liked that person more than people who had held a cup of iced coffee before reading the same description. So, have hot coffee or tea ready in time for the meeting.

Make Sure the Person Sits on a Soft, Comfortable Chair

Sitting comfortably seems to have a similar effect to drinking something hot. When people sit on a hard or uncomfortable chair and are asked to assess another person, they tend to view that person less favorably than when they are sitting on a soft one. Furthermore, people sitting on hard chairs tend to be tougher in negotiations and discussions than people sitting in soft chairs.

Start the Meeting with Small Talk About the Weather If the Weather Is Bad

The weather subconsciously affects our outlook on life. If it is a sunny day, we tend to enjoy greater life satisfaction. If it is rainy, not so much. So, if you have the difficult meeting on a bad-weather day, what to do? Well, experiments show that when people are asked about the weather, its negative impacts on their outlook seems to be blunted. Talking about the weather makes people aware of their feelings about it, so they are less likely to allow it to affect their attitudes.

In addition to these tricks, you should also consider mastering persuasion principles. Dr. Robert Cialdini, author of the extraordinary book *Influence: The Psychology of Persuasion,* is widely regarded as one of the most prominent experts on human influence and persuasion. I would like to share some of the persuasion principles he has identified.

The Contrast Principle

This refers to how we perceive the differences between two things that are presented to us in succession. Simply put, if the second item is different from the first, we will tend to see it as more different than it really is.

Here are some examples of this principle: If you lift a light object and then a heavy object, you will estimate the second object to be heavier than if you had lifted it without first trying the lighter one. Or, if you are talking with a person you think is attractive and are then joined by a less attractive person, the second person will strike you as less attractive than the person really is.

Here's how to apply this principle. If you want a person to go down a certain path—make a decision, accept an approach, pursue a certain action—be deliberate and develop alternatives or choices for the person. For example, based on what you know about the person you want to influence, develop one alternative he or she would most likely view as too demanding and one alternative, the one that you prefer, that seems much less demanding in contrast. When you are having your conversation, start with the demanding alternative and then go through the less demanding one. Chances are he or she will gladly accept the less demanding alternative and feel that you have done him or her a favor.

The Scarcity Principle

Opportunities seem more valuable and attractive to us when their availability is limited. The idea of potential loss plays a large role in human decision-making. People seem to be more motivated by the thought of losing something than by the thought of gaining something of equal value.

Here's how to apply this principle. Explain that a certain proposal, path, solution, or challenge is unavailable or inappropriate for all but a select group of people with a special set of skills or character. The appetite and desire of the person to be part of that select group will most likely be high; people in general want to feel chosen and special and not excluded.

That people tend to be more sensitive to possible losses than to possible gains is one of the best-supported findings in social science. Therefore, it may be worthwhile to switch your emphasis from the benefits of your proposal, ideas, or suggestions to the threat of a wasted opportunity: "Don't miss this chance" or "Here's what you'll miss out on."

The Commitment and Consistency Principle

People have a strong need to appear reliable and consistent. There are three reasons for this: (1) people around us put a high value on consistency because it makes us predictable, which gives them a sense of comfort and control; (2) it reinforces our perception that our life has structure and order; and (3) it saves energy—we don't have to think any more about it once we have made a decision or a commitment. The need to appear or feel that we are reliable, committed, and consistent increases with age.

Here are some examples of this principle in action:

- The bigger the commitment, the more we tend to convince ourselves of its benefits.
- A person will hold more strongly to a commitment made in front of others than to one made in private.
- A written commitment is much stronger than a verbal one.
- A commitment a person makes about himself or herself as a person tends to change the person's self-image and actions.
- A person is more likely to accept a new course of action or a decision if it feels like an extension of a previous commitment.

How to apply this principle:

- Always try to position your advice to a person as the next natural step based on the person's previous decisions and plans.
- Stimulate people to codevelop their individual action plans based on what you need them to do.
- When people have accomplished something really good, such as being extraordinarily courageous, ask them to describe the situation and what they did; this will make it easier for them to achieve similar accomplishments in the future.
- Always strive to make people express what they like, what they don't like, and what they think is important and less important. You can use what they say as positive

affirmations in discussions to make them feel committed and consistent; for example, "I think we are now facing a situation that is related to what you early on expressed concern about and that you said was important."

- When people are hesitant about a decision or what to do, make them write about it. Suggest that they take a step back first and reflect on why it is going to be hard to succeed with the decision or course of action and how they can overcome the difficulty.

31

Develop Your People into Stars

Moderately demanding to implement in your work life

Every year US businesses spend over $60 billion on consultants to help them become more successful. No matter what specific issue the consulting spend is for, it boils down to a handful of underlying themes: (1) make more money by reducing cost and/or increasing revenue, (2) become stronger and more competitive by building abilities that enable the organization to redefine itself in whatever aspect or dimension is relevant, and (3) through all these and other consulting-supported "improvement activities" become a company that attracts and retains the right people.

In my experience, most companies fail with their improvement ambitions, not because their aims were impossible or wrong or that they used the wrong consultants, but because they didn't address what matters to achieve 1, 2, and 3 above: *acting forcefully on the true purpose of leadership at all levels in any type of organization.*

If you are a leader, the approaches I will describe here are your ticket to play in the same league as the few select leaders in the business world who truly understand what leadership is about. These are the leaders who consistently deliver unrivaled business results, who successfully overcome any challenge, and who can overcome inertia to redirect and transform their businesses overnight.

These leaders understand that the businesses or departments they are responsible for *are not about what they produce,* whether it is products, services, or other outputs, such as administrative support to other parts of the organization. They understand that their businesses or departments are solely about *who produces those outputs—their people.*

But even more important, they know that the greatest responsibility they have as leaders is to make sure that all of their direct reports develop their skills and mindsets, and that *they do that in an integrated way in their everyday work.* The leaders focus on one thing only—to turn all their direct reports into star performers, who unleash their unlimited potential through their everyday work.

Why Developing Your Direct Reports Is Your Most Important Leadership Responsibility

Developing your people is your most important responsibility as a leader for three reasons.

First, this is one of the few areas in the professional world where the best interests of the company are completely aligned with the best interests of its people. For you and your direct reports, the benefits of focusing on personal and professional development in everyday work are almost unlimited. As mentioned earlier in the book, working daily to develop yourself leads to increased brain health, which is decisive for both short- and long-term health, performance, and mental well-being.

Do this and the experience of work changes dramatically. Suddenly it gives you more energy than it takes. You will have more fun and look forward to your workday. Leaving work, you will feel a sense of accomplishment, leading to a greater ability to relax and close the books on your day. This will improve your sleep. Furthermore, focusing on developing your skills every day will make you feel stronger and in better control over your situation, leading to less stress. This enables you to produce better results, which leads to greater rewards and the feeling of true achievement.

Altogether, this builds you and your direct reports' ability to shape your destiny by becoming stars at what you do. You will become magnets for bigger and bigger professional opportunities. Why? Because true mastery, as mentioned earlier, never goes out of fashion. People as well as companies always want to "hang with" superstars.

Second, developing yourself and your direct reports is in the best interest of the company. All companies, no matter what the industry or business, must continuously strive to reach ever-higher goals to stay healthy and competitive. The only way to achieve this is to make sure the company's people constantly develop their skills and mindsets, because a company is no more nor less than the sum of its people.

Not acting on this forcefully as a leader or a company would be like an NHL hockey team striving to win the Stanley Cup but investing in equipment (skates, sticks, helmets, Zamboni machines) instead of training and player development. The only sustainable way to reach ever-higher corporate goals is to make sure people constantly develop in their everyday work, because people who do so:

1. Become more engrossed in their tasks, which enables them to develop their intrinsic motivation.
2. Outperform people who don't develop, because they give much more attention to what they do and how they do it. This developmental mindset counteracts the natural tendency of

people to operate purely on habit, which leads to arrested development and gradually deteriorating performance.

3. Continuously formulate more ambitious goals and aspirations than people who don't develop, simply because people who develop continuously realize that there is no limit for what they can achieve and what they can become.

4. Are much more on task than people who don't develop. According to my observations, people who develop spend up to one hour of more productive work per day (which adds up to more than a month of more productive work during a year) than employees who do not feel they are continually developing.

5. Develop greater self-leadership than people who don't develop; for example, they have a greater drive to identify and conduct critical initiatives because they represent opportunities to learn more.

6. Experience less stress and are more rarely ill than people who don't develop—the higher degree of attention and thought leads to a sense of greater autonomy and control over their situation, including a greater ability to deal with uncertainty.

7. Tend to be more cooperative and helpful than people who don't develop, because they like their work. This also makes them much less likely to leave the company.

8. Are extremely open to suggestions of changes they might pursue to further accelerate their development and mastery. People who don't develop tend to be territorial and resistant to people and initiatives that threaten to "rock the boat."

Third, there is no more powerful way to create a healthy bond between you, your direct reports, and their bond with the company than to make sure they are personally and professionally developing. The unique bond this creates is the ultimate reward for a leader. The deep sense of purpose you will experience from observing direct reports grow and accomplish things they did not think they were capable of is unrivaled and cannot be derived from any other experience except parenting.

During my years as an executive and leader I worked for companies that needed to be transformed. My colleagues and I developed approaches to turn the companies around and generate business improvements worth billions of dollars. But that is not what comes to mind when I think about this period in my professional life. What I remember is the work with my own direct reports.

From day one in all my leadership positions, I always insisted that my direct reports put their personal and professional development at the top of the agenda. Every time, I was surprised by how quickly they changed. After only a week or two they performed much better. They became more happy but also more inclined to take on bigger and bigger challenges.

One of strongest memories from this period is a Christmas dinner with twenty of my direct reports. I had been with the company for a year, and this was our first dinner together.

Before food was served, I decided to stand up to share some reflections. I talked about each of them, what they had accomplished, and how they had developed during the year. I could sense it was an emotional moment for them.

Later in the evening, some of them came to me to talk. They had tears in their eyes when they told me that our year together had made them understand how magnificent and fulfilling their work could be. Some of them had been working for the company for twenty-five years and more.

This and many, many similar moments during my time as a leader, and subsequently as a coach, have made my personal and professional journey rewarding beyond anything I could have imagined when I started this journey almost thirty years ago. Furthermore, one thing all these moments have taught me is that it is never too late for anyone to completely rethink his or her approach to work to love doing it.

So, what do you need to make personal and professional development the key priority for you and your direct reports?

First, let me tell you what you don't need. You don't need an expensive IT system to support your efforts. You don't need to hire external experts or consultants. You don't need to radically reprioritize your agenda or how you allocate your time. And you don't need to ask for permission from HR or any other department "responsible" for the guidelines and tools for people development. What I will describe is fully compatible with any type of "system" for personal and professional development your organization has in place.

I'll visualize the approach by describing how one of my clients, Barbara, does it with her direct reports.

Meet Barbara

Barbara is head of operations at a hedge fund in New York City. The operations department is a stressful and demanding work environment where the stakes are high and the pressure is always on, and where bad behaviors—for example, a lack of collaboration and support and a dog-eat-dog mentality—are rife. It is also an environment where systematic approaches to personal and professional development are rarely prioritized or pursued. More often it is sink or swim—you either make it or you're out.

Early on in our coaching, Barbara expressed concerns about her department. She felt that the stress levels were too high, the quality of collaboration and support too low, and that people were not working to unleash their potential for accelerated growth and performance. Retaining people was a challenge, not only in her department but in every department at the hedge fund.

Start by Building Knowledge and Commitment

I advised Barbara to first build solid knowledge with her team of direct reports around intrinsic motivation and personal and professional development. Barbara used different knowledge resources—for example, some of my writings, as well as additional articles and extracts from books—to have both individual conversations and team discussions.

Next, I recommended that she build commitment by developing a team contract. I picked up this approach from a top hockey coach I had worked with a few years back. A team contract defines the behaviors each player needs to adhere to for the team to perform well and reach its goals. In a professional setting such as Barbara's, a team contract can be used to define development goals and as a point of discussion in individual conversations and in team meetings. It can also be used in surveys and discussions with stakeholders that your department is dependent on or serves.

Barbara has eight direct reports. She divided them into two teams of four and tasked them with coming up with five behaviors to ensure that personal and professional development would be a key priority.

Each team developed draft proposals. Barbara then convened a meeting where each team presented its proposals. Three of the behaviors were agreed to. The next step was to develop two additional behaviors. After two weeks, Barbara convened the teams again and they settled on two more behaviors. The behaviors were then formalized in a document that all team members, including Barbara, signed. Posters were also designed that featured the behaviors, so they could be displayed in common areas, conference rooms, and individual workplaces.

The team contract said:

Our Behaviors	Why It Matters
We seek and share excitement every day.	Our work is complex and important. It offers many opportunities to feel excited and energized. If we don't expect to experience excitement in our everyday work, we will not recognize it.
We think before we talk.	We should always speak our mind but do it wisely. Words can either hurt or create. Also, words not based on sufficient facts and good logic risk leading in the wrong direction.
We are always on time.	We adhere to deadlines and meeting times to show each other and our stakeholders respect, as well as to continuously improve our ability to plan our work wisely.
We strive to deliver better than expected.	All our work enables our stakeholders to do their work. Delivering what is expected is a sign of commitment; exceeding expectations is a sign of genuine care and passion.
We grow and develop every day.	Our work offers unlimited opportunities for planning and execution in new and better ways, enabling us to grow our skills and mastery every day.

With her team more knowledgeable and a team contract in place, Barbara was ready for the next step.

Pursue the Three Critical Skills That Drive Intrinsic Motivation and Personal and Professional Development

Besides making it a habit to always focus on exciting outcomes (FEOs) when performing tasks and activities, three skills are critical to enable people to grow and love what they do: problem-solving (or logical thinking, as described earlier in these pages), task management, and self-management.

As mentioned earlier, problem-solving is fundamental for intrinsic motivation, well-being, development, and performance—few things make us feel as alive and strong as when we are solving problems, and few things kill our motivation as much as facing problems we either can't understand or solve. In a professional environment the problem-solving skill is about numerous subskills, for example, quantifying the problem, structuring the problem so it can be understood and solved, dealing with the uncertainty in what you know and don't know about the problem and its solution, and developing robust recommendations for how to deal with it.

Task management is equally important; a key theme of this book is that all tasks and activities offer unlimited opportunities to be performed in new and better ways. Like problem-solving, task management also consists of a handful of subskills, for example, planning, defining measurable outcomes (or FEOs), managing complexity, identifying improvement opportunities, and maintaining a dedication to quality. This deliberate way of thinking about tasks and activities enables intrinsic motivation in our approach to work.

The skill of self-management also contains many subskills, but two of the most important are about mindset and feedback. The mindset skill is to embrace that we can and should always improve how we do things. When we solicit feedback, we gain opportunities for self-improvement and self-knowledge, whether we act on the feedback or not.

To make these skills tangible and so her team could assess themselves, Barbara and I developed descriptions of each of them and displayed them in a chart, in a continuum from mastery (solid) to "needs work" (issues).

Implement Weekly Individual Work and Development FEOs

The next step for Barbara and her team was to agree on a way of working that integrates development and performance. The key requirement was a short-term focus, since that stimulates action, keeps each team member focused on his or her daily performance and development, and ensures that the team and Barbara support one another.

PROBLEM-SOLVING	SOLID	MINOR IMPROVEMENT	CLEAR DEVELOPMENT NEEDS	ISSUES
Quantifying problems and issues	Always securing a solid view on how big a problem or issue is up front before pursuing it.	Quantifying the problem or issue is part of the working process but not always done up front.	Has a good intuition for whether a problem is big or not, but often does not pursue to validate intuition.	Assumes too often how big a problem is without proper analysis.
Issue identification	Has an unusual flair for quickly identifying the most critical aspects of any problem.	Can follow complex, interrelated sets of issues without difficulty. Most often identifies the most critical issues to address.	Has clear, logical approach to the issues but struggles with identifying the most critical ones.	Issue focus and logic of problem-solving approach is not readily apparent.
Dealing with uncertainty	Always able to break down insights to a problem into what's certain/known, what's based on beliefs, and what is unknown and acts to reduce the level of uncertainty in a balanced way.	Most often quickly develops a good view of what is known and unknown about a problem. Can sometimes lean too much on assumptions or beliefs rather than facts.	Can identify unknown aspects of a problem but needs support in addressing those aspects efficiently.	Tends to be "all over the place." Is most often overly confident about what the problem is and how to solve it, and/or reacts negatively when facing uncertainty.
Problem structuring	Structures ill defined, vague problems, allowing the team to undertake problem-solving in a focused way.	Structures complex problems with normal support needed; sees several ways to structure the problem and understands the pros and cons of each.	Identifies key issues and does a solid job structuring problem-solving but most often with the need of continuous iteration and support.	Needs significant help in structuring problem-solving approaches.
Analytical skills and approach	Pushes beyond existing analytic capabilities; builds new conceptual and/or analytic approaches.	Recognizes the need for, draws on, and rapidly learns new analytic approaches.	Is a good analyst but does not identify needs for new analytical approaches.	Still has some shortfalls in analytic skills and difficulty in embracing new analytical approaches.

TASK MANAGEMENT	SOLID	MINOR IMPROVEMENT	CLEAR DEVELOPMENT NEEDS	ISSUES
Response to problem shifts	Leads team to manage such changes; effectively leverages judgment base of people who know more about the problem.	Most of the time handles shifting problems and issues; able to integrate new findings into work.	Is ill at ease as the problems and issues shift over time, but recognizes the need to shift.	"Fights" adjusting the course of the work when issues change.
Developing recommendations	Develops recommendations that can pragmatically be implemented.	Most often develops a solid set of thorough recommendations.	Sees *so whats* and, with help and some support, develops thorough recommendations.	Recommendations are often incomplete and/or do not clearly build on the relevant findings.
Planning	Can structure efficient plans to address complex problems and priorities.	Can rapidly complete solid, targeted plans to address familiar problems and priorities.	Does a solid job of laying out a plan but requires support.	Tends not to do thoughtful planning and/or cannot complete a plan without much assistance.
Developing clear and measurable outcomes/FEOs	Always developing clear and measurable outcomes up front to enable pragmatic plans and task prioritization.	Developing clear and measurable outcomes up front to guide overall planning (but not on detail level).	Always striving to define clear outcomes but struggles to make them measurable.	Does not think in outcomes but in activities and tasks. Low ability to prioritize within an activity or plan.
Managing complexity	Manages complex, rapidly moving projects and still has time to think beyond the task of managing the project; delivers value beyond the scope of the project.	Comfortably manages complex projects without missing any commitments.	Comfortably manages straightforward projects but sometimes struggles with deadlines.	Has difficulty managing projects to meet deadlines.

SELF-MANAGEMENT	SOLID	MINOR IMPROVEMENT	CLEAR DEVELOPMENT NEEDS	ISSUES
Improvement focus	Continuously identifies areas for thoughtful improvement and change. Pursues improvements and change in a structured way with clear outcomes and plans. Sees possibilities instead of obstacles.	Often makes suggestions for thoughtful improvement and change and is prepared to drive them. Is positive to trying out new ideas.	Sometimes makes suggestions for thoughtful improvement and change but procrastinates in pursuing them and/or trying out new ideas.	Rarely comes up with ideas for thoughtful changes and improvements. Is not willing to try out new ideas. Sees obstacles rather than possibilities.
Dedication to quality	Delivers high-quality work that exceeds requirements. There is no need to review deliveries. Is open-minded to improving quality standards.	Delivers quality work that sometimes exceeds requirements. There is normally no need for reviewing but is open-minded toward performance reviews.	Fulfills quality requirements but needs some support. Deliverables must be reviewed.	The quality requirements are not fulfilled.
Sequencing	Shows strong ability to identify the critical order in which to pursue all tasks within any given project or assignment.	Most often shows ability to identify the critical order in which to pursue own tasks.	Understands the need for identifying the critical order in which to pursue own tasks within the specific assignment but needs guidance in how to go about it.	Often confused by the complexity of tasks in any assignment.
Mindset	Sees every task and situation as an opportunity to innovate and grow.	Clear focus on development but at times too much focus on areas only relevant for own career.	Pursues development, but can easily be discouraged by failures in own development efforts.	Weak focus on own development. Inflates value of own strengths.
Acting on feedback and seeking support	Proactively seeks and acts on structured as well as in-the-moment feedback and support from team, peers, and people exposed to own work.	Open to and acts on feedback and seeks support proactively when facing challenges.	Most often open to feedback but procrastinates in turning feedback into action.	Does not seek feedback frequently and hesitates to seek support and timely help when needed.

After two to three team discussions, they decided on the following way of working:

1. Every Friday, each team member spends fifteen to twenty minutes to define his or her most important three to five individual weekly work FEOs, including at least one weekly FEO addressing one of the three critical skills (problem-solving, task management, and self-management).
2. Every workday, team members spend fifteen to twenty minutes to reflect on their progress working toward their weekly FEOs, including rating their day on a scale of 1–10 (10 = great).
3. The eight team members were paired into four peer apprenticeship teams, who meet for thirty-plus minutes every Friday or Monday to support and learn from each other about the past week and coming week's FEOs.
4. Once a month all eight team members meet with Barbara to share and learn from one another about their performance and development over the month.

Barbara worked in the same way with her weekly FEOs and daily reflections. In addition, she started a simple daily log in which she wrote down any observations of team members she could potentially share with them as feedback.

On alternating weeks, Barbara joined a peer apprenticeship team at their weekly thirty-plus meeting and had a thirty-minute-plus one on one with a team member.

The only thing Barbara needed to do to get this way of working going was to develop a template for her and her team members to use. Here's the template they developed—with a real example from one of Barbara's team members:

WEEKLY PLAN	DAILY 15-MINUTE REFLECTION—Achievements, Challenges, and Insights per Weekly FEO					
Critical Skills FEO	**Monday**	**Tuesday**	**Wednesday**	**Thursday**	**Friday**	**Fulfillment**
Improve task management with focus on cutting time to execute (one task every day).	Monthly 1:1 calls with 8 of the portfolio managers cut from 20 to 10 minutes by reporting progress much crisper.	Managed to cut 30 minutes in designing graphs for portfolio manager presentation.	Was not able to cut time executing any task today. Had to wait for input from others, which delayed my analysis work.	Cut time in half for reading monthly report on operational risk, still managed to summarize key insights to share in an email with the team.	Managed to cut my prep time with 30 minutes for Monday's team meeting while actually making what I want to share even clearer.	80%

Key Work FEOs	**Monday**	**Tuesday**	**Wednesday**	**Thursday**	**Friday**	**Fulfillment**
Finalize presentation for portfolio management meeting by Wednesday instead of Friday this week.	Drafted a good story line and tested it with Barbara, who liked it.	Made a complete draft of the presentation, sent to Barbara for approval. Good input from her, was able to finalize the presentation in less than one hour.	Sent presentation out to portfolio managers at 9:00 A.M. today—two days earlier than required, which gives them extra time to prepare.			100%

Get complete buy-in from Bob Stevenson to perform model risk assessments in the new way.		Tested my key arguments with three people close to Bob, got pushback on one of the arguments.	Went back to test refined arguments with the three people. Got advice to let Bob speak his mind before I introduce my arguments.	Finalized the three-slide deck for Friday meeting with Bob. Feels short and crisp, and clear in what the ask is of Bob.	Working lunch with Bob: He bought into my arguments but wants to think more about how to pursue his implementation until coming Tuesday.	90%
Get agreement from portfolios managers Steve and Jane on timing and approach to their ask to onboard new counterparty to their platform.	Sent a brief description of the approach to Steve and Jane with the three questions I want them to specifically think about. We will talk on Friday.				Steve and Jane like the approach but want us to rethink the timing of the approach since this is an urgent matter. Will discuss with team and Barbara. Promised to come back to them no later than coming Wednesday.	60%
How was my day? (Rate on scale 1–10 and give a one-sentence explanation)	6 (was a bit fragmented)	8 (felt good progress overall)	5 (not happy to have to push my analysis)	8 (happy to have finalized the presentation)	7 (a good day and a sense of having had a good week)	A better-than-average week

Estimated Time Investment and Benefits

The most common objection leaders have about working in this way is *time*. "How will I have time for this?" What they are asking is, "How will I have time to lead and develop my direct reports?" They might as well be asking how they will have time to do their job as a leader, since leading and developing direct reports drives all aspects of the business.

The time investment is not that daunting. Here's how it breaks down:

For each of Barbara's team members per month:

- Defining the weekly FEOs = 20 minutes x 4 = 80 minutes
- Weekly peer apprenticeship meeting = 30 minutes x 4 = 120 minutes
- Daily reflections = 75 minutes a week x 4 = 300 minutes
- Biweekly one on one with Barbara = 30 minutes x 2 = 60 minutes
- Monthly team meeting = 60 minutes

Total time required: 620 minutes or approximately ten hours per month, which is less than 7 percent of total work time over an entire year. What a deal! What other way of working enables your direct reports to get great support from their peers and from their leader, while monitoring and learning from their own progress and development?

What about Barbara's time investment? Here it is:

- Defining the weekly FEOs = 20 minutes x 4 = 80 minutes
- Participation in peer apprenticeship meetings biweekly = 30 minutes x 8 = 240 minutes
- Daily reflections = 75 minutes a week x 4 = 300 minutes

- Biweekly one on one with each team = 30 minutes x 16 = 480 minutes
- Monthly team meeting = 60 minutes

This makes the total time investment for Barbara around 1,200 minutes or twenty hours a month. This is less than 15 percent of her total working time during a year. Another deal of a lifetime! What other way of working with such a minor time investment can enable you to live up to your prime responsibility as a leader—to lead and to *develop all your direct reports*? But look at the benefits Barbara and other leaders have enjoyed working in this or similar ways with their direct reports:

- Barbara quickly got perfect control over what was happening in her department and among her team members' areas of responsibilities.
- Her ability to retain the right people improved markedly.
- Her team members' self-leadership noticeably increased, which freed up a lot of time for her.
- Discussing, agreeing on, and successfully executing necessary improvements and change initiatives become a natural part of everyday work.
- Difficult conversations and conflicts were rapidly reduced.
- Skills such as defining clear and exciting outcomes, planning, risk assessment, problem-solving, prioritization, time management, and self-management all improved.

Barbara's ability to understand each of her team members, their true strengths, development needs, and aspirations, also improved, which enabled her to do what far too many leaders fail to: delegate more of her own tasks as development opportunities for her team members.

Delegating Tasks as Development Opportunities

I delegated my tasks as one of the key development approaches for my direct reports, including inviting them to take my place at the executive team meeting from time to time.

Barbara was hesitant at first, so we spent a lot of time talking about how to do it in the right way. I explained that the true challenge with successfully delegating a task is the leaders themselves. Often they lack a clear idea of what the desired or required work results should be and are clueless about how they perform the task themselves as they just do it on autopilot. The way to do it right is to know how you would do the task yourself so you can coach your report through it, and to be clear about what measurable or tangible outcome is required.

I coached Barbara to use this three-step approach for delegating:

Step 1: Spend fifteen to twenty minutes (or more time if it is a big and complicated task, e.g., to lead an initiative) to think through how you would execute the task yourself.

Push or clarify your thinking by writing down your answers to the following questions:

1. What is the desired or required outcome of the task, that is, what work result needs to be created?
2. In what overall steps should the task be executed?
3. For each step, what are the most important as well as most difficult tasks?
4. What should be the timing of each step?
5. What is a good work result in each step?

Step 2: Talk to the team member you intend to delegate the task to. Ask the person to spend fifteen to twenty minutes to answer questions two through five above concerning the task.

Have the person write down his or her answers to secure clarity of thinking and dialogue between you.

Step 3: Sit down with the direct report and run through his or her answers together.

Now you will be able to:

1. See where you and your direct report are aligned on how the task should be executed and where you have gaps.
2. Instantly give guidance and steer the person right from the beginning.
3. Learn something about the person's strengths and development needs.
4. Plan your support for the person's apprenticeship in a smart way.

If the gaps are too big, perhaps it is too soon to delegate this task. But at least you will have learned something about your direct report, which can give you insights into other approaches you can use to help the person develop.

In Conclusion

Contrary to popular beliefs, developing your employees is neither difficult nor terribly time-consuming.

Use the tools and approaches Barbara and other leaders have used. I promise you will not regret it.

32

Guide Your Company to Succeed at What It Is Most Likely Terrible At: Leading Change

Moderately demanding to implement in your work life

As mentioned, a lot of money and time are spent formulating strategies, goals, and plans to drive smaller or larger changes or "transformations" in the professional world. But they seldom work, making change efforts by far the biggest and most persistent enigmas in the business world.

Why is transformation so hard? Are companies using the wrong goals and strategies? Do their executives feel the goals are not important? Do they lack plans for working toward them? Do they require skills, experience, or time they don't have? The simple answer is no.

The basic reason is that most organizations don't have a clue about how to drive the execution of their goals and strategies in a way that engages their people. Another way to put that is that they don't act forcefully on the true purpose of leadership, which is to make sure that all employees develop their skills and mindsets, and that they do it in a way that is seamlessly integrated into their daily work.

Succeeding with change is not that complicated if you know how the human mind operates. You need to secure three preconditions.

First, Choose Your Words Wisely

People tend to fear change because it has often meant negative things for them in the past, putting them in situations that were even more confusing than the one that was being fixed, or costing them their jobs. Calling change *change* puts you in an uphill battle from the start. *Development,* on the other hand, carries a strong connotation of productive, healthy growth. We perceive it as good and positive because it makes us stronger and we feel we have some control over the process.

So, stop talking about *change* and start talking about *development* or, preferably, *our natural next step.* Thinking and talking in terms of *our natural next step* leads to a new and better world of thoughts both for the people who will be involved in the development work and the people who will be affected by it. It takes the drama out of what will be done and helps to make it feel like more of an attractive way forward. The *next natural step* also promotes a balanced view of everything that is good in the current state and everything that can become better or be developed in the next.

Just changing one word allows you to manage and increase your impact exponentially.

Second, Work Diligently to Answer the Three Universal Questions

Companies often invest too little in detailed descriptions of how people's actual work will change when they begin change or development initiatives. By *detailed,* I mean that every leader and employee should know exactly which areas should be developed—but equally important, what will *not* change.

As the leader of a development effort, you should be able to answer the three universal questions people ask when faced with something new: (1) What will I gain? (2) What will I lose? (3) What will I keep?

Also, bear in mind that people suffer twice as much from a loss as they feel excited over something they gain, and that is particularly the case if they lose some kind of freedom or privilege. When you introduce a development effort, be sure to structure your communications so they address each of the three questions in a positive way:

- What you will continue to do in the same way and what you will do in a new way, and why, when, and how this will happen.
- What you will stop doing, and why, when, and how this will happen.
- What you will start doing, and why, when, and how this should happen.

Third, Make People Feel Ownership

Like any other project, development work stands or falls depending on the quality of the preparation that you put into it, and the most important thing you can do at the outset is *make people feel ownership of the required work*. If you do that well, you will leverage the Ikea effect—our tendency to place a disproportionately high value on objects we had a hand in assembling. This includes not just furniture, but anything we've made a personal investment in, including ideas, beliefs, and ways of working (regardless of their quality).

Here is a simple and powerful way to do that. I have used this approach many times and coach my clients to use it. It creates a much faster and more positive momentum around whatever change or development initiative you need to pursue.

Let's say you want to implement a new way of working in your department.

Step 1: Write an easy-to-read document that clearly lays out the new way of working. No jargon: clear and to the point. Make sure it covers the following topics:

- What is the new way of working?
- What tangible benefits will the individual and the department get from working in this new way? If you don't have firsthand experience with it, interview people who have and attach their testimonials.
- How will a typical workday or workweek look when the new ways of working are implemented? If you talk to people who have experience in this, share their stories and perspectives.
- What are the typical things people will need to (1) continue doing, (2) stop doing, and (3) start doing to gain the full benefits of working in this new way?

Step 2: Share the document with all those in your department and ask them to think through and write down answers to the following questions:

- What personal and professional benefits do I want to experience by mastering this new way of working?
- What in my current approach to my work should I *continue* doing, since it is in line with this new way of working and the benefits I want to get?
- What should I *stop* doing since it is not in line with this new way of working and the benefits I want to get?
- What don't I do today that I should start doing to be in line with this new way of working and the benefits I want to reap?

- What support would I need to stop doing and start doing things in these new ways?
- Which parts of this new way of working are the hardest to understand or accept? Why?

By asking people to think through and answer these questions, you leverage both the Ikea effect and the commitment and consistency principle: people have a strong need to appear consistent in their beliefs. A written commitment is much stronger than a verbal one.

Step 3: Arrange a joint learning and work session with all people in the department.

The main work and learning should take place among the participants—you should not give a lecture or try to lead a discussion with a big group of people. Everyone needs to be highly active.

One reason for this is that the more people talk and perform actual work—for example, problem-solving—the more ownership they will feel, and the more likely the event will be perceived as a positive emotional experience. The other reason has to do with learning: when we talk, write, and work through a task, we create much stronger neural structures.

The main content of this work and learning session should be based on the prework the participants have done; that is, the answers that they have written to your questions.

At the beginning of the session, divide the participants into groups or teams of three or more, depending on how many participants there are.

As the first set of work, give them twenty-five minutes to name their team, define a credo, and assign a set of team roles. These actions increase the sense of ownership and team spirit, making the session more fun. One of the roles is that of team leader, who is responsible for making sure the team solves their tasks on time. The teams should also select someone to be the presenter of the team's findings. A third member can act as the fact gatherer, that is, someone who goes to other teams and asks for advice and input during their teamwork.

When the full group reconvenes, each team should spend five minutes to present their team's name, credo, and how their roles have been assigned and why. Then the group breaks up again so the teams can begin their two sessions. In each, the teams build on the work they did as individuals, when they responded to the change document in writing. Now they are answering these questions as a group.

Teamwork 1—discuss and align the team based on individual answers:

- What personal and professional benefits do I want to experience by mastering this new way of working?
- What in my approach to my work today should I *continue* doing?
- What do I do today in how I approach my work that I should *stop* doing?
- What should I *start* doing?

Teamwork 2—discuss and align in team, based on individual answers:

- What support would I need to stop doing and start doing the things needed?
- What parts of this new way of working are most hard to understand? Why?
- How would my plan look if I start to work in this new way?

- With the support of the other team members, each member plans his or her next individual steps for the continue/stop/start behaviors and habits, as well as for how to learn more about the new way of working.

Step 4: Keep the teams in place after the work and learning session. Now they are working and apprenticeship teams, providing mutual support as the change gets underway. Keeping the teams together has other benefits as well. First, it leverages peer pressure to reinforce the new habits and behaviors. Second, it allows you and your department to monitor and report on your progress and any challenges you are facing. These can be discussed and addressed at subsequent department-wide gatherings.

The secret is to reserve enough time to work on each of the three preconditions I have described. Most often, companies operate on the unreflective idea that they need to move into action quickly, only to realize that nothing or little is achieved. Be careful about language, detailed in your answers to the three universal questions, and drive a hands-on process to make certain that people feel ownership of it.

33

Get Your Good Ideas Accepted and Implemented

Demanding to implement in your work life

Do you feel that your organization is not open to new ideas and creativity? Well, chances are that your organization is like most other organizations I have encountered—they have spent gazillions of dollars on ideas and projects that did not deliver on their promises to create value.

Achieving success with new ideas and projects seems to be a universal problem for companies. Why? Poor execution and follow-up is common. But even more common are poor ideas or, at least, poor and incomplete work in qualifying the ideas.

In this chapter, I share a bulletproof approach to make sure that your idea will not only be great, but that it will be accepted by decision makers and executed successfully.

I first developed this approach in 2008, when the CIO at a large company asked me to help him and his team improve the precision of the technology projects in their multimillion-dollar project portfolio. At the time, fewer than 50 percent of them were meeting time, budget, and value delivery objectives.

Before we started the work, I identified a few companies that appeared to have an impeccable track record of successful completion of all types of projects on these metrics. One was a global financial institution that industry experts had for several years running singled out as one of the best managed in the world. Through my network, I secured a meeting with its chief operating officer.

My first question to the COO was about how they approached new ideas and potential projects. His answer completely threw me off: "That is such a complex issue. If we can avoid adopting new ideas and projects, we certainly prefer that. In our experience, skepticism, as well as a laser focus on the risks with every new idea or project, is the key to success."

Fair enough, I thought. By focusing on the weaknesses of a new idea or potential project, you avoid being carried away by the enthusiasm of the people proposing it. My next question was how the company dealt with ideas or potential projects that did seem good and relevant. The COO leaned back and answered, "That is a cumbersome process. If an idea seems good, then a detailed process starts where all the departments that are supposed to benefit from the idea are engaged to discuss whether they believe they will benefit from it or not, and if they believe they will, exactly how. But that is just the first step. The next is to figure out how to fund it. All the departments that would benefit from the idea should finance their part of it. But since every department is different and will receive different levels of benefits, there must be a rigorous analysis of how to allocate the costs."

The hour I spent with the COO taught me a lot about the factors for qualifying good ideas and setting them up for success. It's important to appreciate the enthusiasm of people who bring new ideas and projects, but the initial focus should be on their weaknesses. If an idea or project seems good, over-invest in qualifying the gain with the departments that would theoretically benefit from it. Make sure they will finance their part of it in a way that is commensurate with those benefits.

This is important for two reasons: First, if the departments finance their part of the project, they have skin in the game, and they are more likely to do their part to make it succeed. Second, if the cost for each department is correlated with the benefits it will get, the allocation of costs will be viewed as fair. This reduces resistance and cynicism. The key learning is that you should try to make it *really hard* for people to suggest ideas for potential projects. The ideas and projects that emerge will thus have legs and be much more valuable and realistic.

Energized with the wisdom from the COO, I got started with the CIO who had engaged me. After about six months we had developed a completely new approach for how ideas for potential technology projects should be developed and qualified.

This illustration summarizes what had to be in place before considering an IT investment:

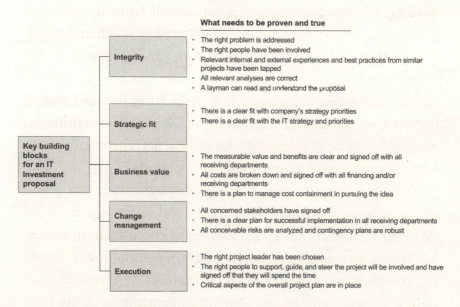

	What needs to be proven and true
Integrity	• The right problem is addressed • The right people have been involved • Relevant internal and external experiences and best practices from similar projects have been tapped • All relevant analyses are correct • A layman can read and understand the proposal
Strategic fit	• There is a clear fit with company's strategy priorities • There is a clear fit with the IT strategy and priorities
Business value	• The measurable value and benefits are clear and signed off with all receiving departments • All costs are broken down and signed off with all financing and/or receiving departments • There is a plan to manage cost containment in pursuing the idea
Change management	• All concerned stakeholders have signed off • There is a clear plan for successful implementation in all receiving departments • All conceivable risks are analyzed and contingency plans are robust
Execution	• The right project leader has been chosen • The right people to support, guide, and steer the project will be involved and have signed off that they will spend the time • Critical aspects of the overall project plan are in place

Key building blocks for an IT Investment proposal

To even propose a project, it had to have been thoroughly vetted on its integrity (meaning it addressed the right problem and brought the right people and the right resources to bear on it), its strategic fit and business value, and its viability (meaning that all the relevant stakeholders were on board to develop and steer the project through implementation).

In the twenty-four months after implementing the new approach, the CIO and the company increased the performance of their technology projects from fewer than 50 percent delivered on time, on budget, and with the expected value capture to 92 percent. They also got about 10 percent more value out of their bigger projects compared to what was originally estimated. Furthermore, it became radically easier to weed out irrelevant project proposals, and the number of such proposals declined over time.

The CIO got invitations from several companies and associations to give speeches about how the company managed to improve so much. After a few years, he left the company to build an advisory business around the approach. Later, he became a successful venture capitalist.

Your Benefits from Using This Approach

Before I describe the approach in detail, I want to elaborate on the benefits it will give you, even beyond strengthening your idea, making it more attractive for decision makers, and enabling successful execution.

1. It is fun and rewarding.
2. It will enable you to understand the people and departments in your organization much better.
3. It will sharpen your analytical skills.
4. It will give you ample opportunities to practice and develop your social skills.

5. It will build your reputation and network in the organization.

Here is the step-by-step approach.

Embrace Four Success Factors

Before you begin, consider these four factors, each of which will improve your chances of success:

1. **Involve a seasoned and business-oriented professional from the finance department from the outset.** Not only will you get all the help you need for your financial analyses, it will help you position your idea in the broader business and financial context. Finance people understand your organization's governance model, and who the relevant decision makers are.

2. **Engage all relevant people in the creation of your idea.** That includes three categories of people: (a) those who should benefit from the idea, (b) those who can help improve the idea, and (c) those who will decide on the idea. The most common mistake professionals make when proposing ideas is that they only talk to the decision makers, not the people who would benefit from the idea or could make it even better. During development, plan for at least two well-structured meetings with all those who would benefit from your idea and use the meetings to align people on the benefits, costs, and what needs to change to capture full value. Also, spend a lot of time researching people who have pursued similar ideas and learn as much from them as you can.

3. **Be driven by a mindset that says, "Perhaps this idea is not so great after all."** This secures common sense and critical

and logical thinking in every step of the process. The more you focus on the weaknesses of your idea, the more solid your idea will be (unless it is useless, but then you will save a lot of time and energy, since you will quickly realize that and pull the plug).

4. **Write your proposal in plain and simple language.** That way anyone can understand it, even if the person is not a part of the functional area of the company your idea addresses.

Just adhering to these four factors helps create a culture of greater transparency and collaboration. One area that tangibly improved in the company I advised was the collaboration between line managers, finance people, and technology professionals.

Start by Proving Your Idea Is Good Business

Next, invest a lot of time up front outlining crisply and clearly your idea and its relevance to the business. Be specific; quantify your idea's business value wherever possible, preferably in dollars and cents. Proposing ill-defined ideas such as "improve our processes," "fix the quality," "implement software Y," or "buy company X" is simply not acceptable. If your idea is to adopt a software product, you need to describe what you want to achieve by implementing this idea; for example, "We should invest $3 million in software X for our call center in Nevada to reduce customer churn by 15 percent."

When you have formulated your idea in a specific and relevant way by working with the appropriate finance person, you should then identify all those who would benefit from your idea and have structured individual meetings with them.

The purpose of these meetings should be to discuss how

the overall benefits and costs of your idea break down by department. The meeting should cover the following topics:

- The introduction of your idea and its estimated overall benefits and costs.
- The benefits the specific department could reap from the idea.
- How your idea will fit the overall agenda and priorities in the specific department.
- A stress test to determine if these benefits could be created by doing something else, and if so, at what cost?

Each department should sign off on both the benefits it will receive and the costs it will carry for the project in order to secure traceability and transparency in the value creation as well as costs; create ownership and commitment among the receiving line managers and with it pull; avoid tension and conflicts between the project and the people who will implement and manage it; simplify work planning; and minimize the risk of duplicated efforts and non-value-adding activities.

If you and your finance person get sign-offs from all the people or departments affected, then you should have your first meeting with the decision makers. The purpose of this meeting is *not* to get them to say yes, no, or maybe. It is simply to introduce your idea and get feedback.

Smart decision makers typically zoom in on these questions: "Is this really the best idea to solve this problem or achieve this business objective? What other alternatives exist?" For most people who bring an idea to the table, this feels like a complete turnoff. Why? Because most people who bring ideas to the table are in love with their ideas. They can't understand why they should consider alternatives when their idea is so fantastic. You, on the other hand, have this covered since you have talked with each department about alternative ideas as well as made sure that your idea fits with their overall agendas and priorities.

If there is more than one decision maker, you should have individual meetings with them. *Do not* meet them all together; it will be much easier for you to describe your idea to one person than to a group. The feedback you get from each person will also be much more exhaustive and detailed. Furthermore, the more intimate setting of an individual meeting gives you greater insight into how each decision maker thinks, which will strengthen your ability to communicate with and influence them going forward.

Prove That the Idea Is Doable

You'll need to prove a lot of things before you can claim that your company could and should pursue your idea. The obvious things are that your idea is legal and compliant; that it is in line with corporate strategies and priorities; and that the company has the time and resources to invest.

One way to marshal your proof is to bring in people with experience developing and pursuing similar ideas. For example, if the idea is "We should invest $3 million in software X for our call center," identify people who have experience implementing software X in call centers. If software X is new to your company, you need to source people in other companies that use it. I recommend that you identify at least two projects in different contexts that are similar to yours.

When you and your finance person meet with people with similar experiences, ask them these questions:

- What was the business objective for their idea or project?
- What steps did they take to implement the project?

- For each step, what were the biggest challenges and risks?
- How did they deal with each challenge and risk?
- What were the actual results of the project? Did it meet its business objective?
- What, if anything, would they do differently if they were to pursue the project today?
- What skills, experience, and competence should the ideal leader for this project have?

You will be surprised how much knowledge you will gain.

Now you and your finance person are ready for your next meeting with the people and departments that would benefit from your idea. The agenda for this meeting should cover the following questions:

- What needs to be changed in the department to reap the benefits of the project? For example:
  - Redesign of tasks
  - Redesign of workflows
  - Redesign of roles and responsibilities
  - Improvements of mindsets, behaviors, and skills
  - Other changes
- What would the overall approach, project setup, and plan look like to address these changes?
- What are the risks and challenges, including that people in the department will be stretched for time and attention?
- What insights and experiences from others who have pursued similar ideas are relevant for us?

The end product of each of these meetings should be a handshake on an overall plan for how to pursue your idea successfully in each department.

If you will not lead the potential project, now you need to

source a project leader. The first step is to create a brief description of the idea, listing the skills, experiences, and competence a project leader would need. Show the description to all relevant parties in your company that might know someone who would fit, for example human resources and the people responsible for talent management. When you have identified the names of two or three candidates, you are ready for the last step.

Your Presentation to the Decision Makers

Write a two-to-four-page document in plain and simple language—do not use PowerPoint! The document should simply summarize your idea, following this structure and story line:

1. On the cover page, start with your idea and the measurable business value it will create.
2. The first headline should be "The Idea Is Based on a Solid Business Case." Here you summarize the overall benefits and costs as well as how these are broken down by the affected departments. Explain how the idea fits with the company's overall agenda and priorities.
3. The second headline is "We Can Do It." Under it, you summarize what you have learned from people who pursued similar ideas, the required changes in each department and how to deal with them, and the risks that will need to be managed and how to do that. Also mention your candidates to lead the project.
4. The third headline is "There Are No Better Alternatives, Including Doing Nothing." Here you go through the potential negative effects of not pursuing your idea as well as why other ideas as well as alternative ways to pursue the same business value aren't as good and beneficial as yours.

List all the people that have had a part of developing your idea and the role they have had.

Then send the document to the decision makers as pre-reading and ask them to bring feedback to the meeting. Make sure to have a brief chat with each of them before the final meeting where a decision will be taken.

Build and Maintain Your Own Checklist for Qualifying and Developing Your Ideas

Based on your experience and what you have learned in this chapter, build, continuously develop, and maintain a checklist so you can identify feasible ideas more accurately and develop them into something people are excited to pursue faster and more efficiently.

Here is a starting point:

My idea	We should invest in better X
Main questions	Example of detail questions
Is this a good and relevant idea?	**Business benefits:** Does it support our strategy and critical priorities? Does it enable increased revenue? Does it enable decreased spending, e.g., does it save money on hardware, software, etc.? Does it save time and resources through increased efficiency? Does it deliver/enable more services? Does it enable better quality? If so, what are the costs of quality problems today and the value of improved quality? Does it deliver other benefits, e.g., reputation building? **Investment required:** How much money needs to be spent? How much time and resources must be spent by all involved people? Are there any other costs, for example, opportunity costs in pursuing this idea instead of another? Is the total cost significantly lower than the sum of the business benefits?

My idea	We should invest in better X
Main questions	**Example of detail questions**
Can we pursue the idea?	Is the timing right? That is, can we execute while maintaining focus on our other priorities or down-prioritize other things in a good way? Are all the stakeholders aligned and committed to supporting the execution of the idea? Do we have the competence and experience required to successfully execute the idea? Have we executed similar ideas before, and can we learn from them what worked and what didn't? Do we know all the risks and challenges in executing the idea? Do we have a believable plan for how to execute the idea in an efficient way, including how to contain the costs and monitor the business benefits?
Are there no other alternatives?	Are there other ways than pursuing this idea that could yield the same or better business benefits? Could this idea be integrated in ongoing work in a smart and nondisruptive way instead of as a stand-alone project? Should people other than us execute this idea, either because they are better suited or this would offer them a development opportunity?

Be Dead Serious About Diversity

Demanding to implement in your work life

When people talk about discrimination in the professional world, most often they are referring to prejudices regarding race, ethnicity, and gender. While this type of discrimination exists and should not be tolerated, the kinds of discrimination I describe below are much more common and thus represent an even bigger problem for the long-term health of teams and organizations.

I have worked with thousands of leaders and professionals at more than a hundred organizations. Here's a typical situation I find. A client leads a team with ten team members. He has an especially close and productive relationship with three of them, who generally perform well. But when I dig a little deeper to understand why the relationship with these three team members is as good as it is, it often turns out that it has nothing to do with their performance, but rather with who they are and how they behave. They are either similar to the leader in their personalities or are reliable allies that he can always count on to agree with him. The leader has frequent dialogues with these three members, which may look good on the surface, but can create many problems—not least because the other seven members of the team feel shut out.

The leader's relationship with four of those other team members is neutral, meaning it is neither especially good nor bad. But the leader has a poor relationship with the other three. From his perspective, they have negative attitudes, perform or behave badly, and frequently break with the team norms, but I generally find that this is not true. The real reason for the poor relationship is that these team members are different from the leader and the other team members in how they think or express themselves. Both their needs and their potential contributions to the team are different from those the leader can naturally understand, satisfy, and leverage.

This is the nature of the most common discrimination that takes place in the professional world: a default leadership mode that is more focused on preserving the status quo than evolving it. If leaders and teams view someone as being different in one way—the person's way of speaking, say—that influences their views of all the person's other attributes.

I have observed this type of discrimination on teams whose members are a mix of ethnicities and genders, and on more ethnically homogenous teams. As worthwhile a goal as it is, ensuring a diversity of race, ethnicity, or gender will not address this fundamental problem.

You should be serious about true diversity—that is, being able to leverage different kinds of people's ideas, temperaments, needs, motivations, aspirations, backgrounds, experiences, and ways of communicating—for three reasons.

The first is paramount: to avoid groupthink, which is the tendency to do (or believe) things simply because many other people do (or believe) the same. This is one of the most dangerous brain biases in a professional environment. When everyone is thinking the same, nobody is thinking much. Groupthink kills the unusual, whether in people, experiences, or ideas, starving the organization's gene pool of the diversity it requires to evolve.

The second reason is equally important: to develop your team's and your own social skills. Few things develop people's social skills as much as engaging with people who are different from themselves. If you develop team members with great social skills, you will have secured a great advantage.

The third reason is obvious to most of us (if we are honest with ourselves): it is fundamentally boring and soulless to spend day in and day out with people who are just like ourselves. If I was forced to spend time only with people like me, I would die of ennui. I can't think of a more terrifying scenario than being surrounded by Stefan Falk clones. One of me is more than enough.

Implement the Four Behaviors That Enable Diversity

Fundamentally, what allows or destroys diversity are the thought patterns and behaviors people display. I would therefore recommend that you inculcate thought patterns and behaviors in your team that will unlock their existing differences, while at the same time making it easier for you to recruit new members whose insights and experiences will potentially strengthen your team and allow it to evolve.

I've found four social behaviors that create an environment in which all team members' potential is fully leveraged. These behaviors manifest some of the tools and principles already described in the book, and the best professionals all model them. You, your team, and your colleagues should strive to do so as well.

1. **Leave your inner voice at home. Always do what is in the best interest of the company.** When you bring your selfish needs to work, you inevitably leave much of your intelligence behind. Being consciously or subconsciously

governed by your selfish needs gives you tunnel vision, as you will register only the elements of your situation that are related to those needs. This bias will permeate everything you do: how you perform your tasks, how you engage with your colleagues and stakeholders, and what you will learn. Furthermore, having your selfish needs at work causes negative stress. Why? Simply because you will take everything that doesn't meet your needs as a personal affront. You will most likely leave work every day feeling frustrated, angry, and unfulfilled, burdened by negative thoughts about people who, like you, allowed themselves to be governed by their selfish needs.

2. **Treat everyone you work with as an asset with unlimited potential.** Know that every person you meet in your work has unlimited potential, no matter what the person's current performance. The idea of talent as something that some people have and others lack exists only in the mind of lazy and biased people who want to make it easy for themselves by prejudging. Try to learn something from at least one person every day. When you experience tension in a relationship with a colleague, approach the person and try to resolve the issue proactively. Never talk about colleagues behind their back.

3. **Always stick to the facts.** Trusting your past experience is not enough; you need to make sure you securely understand the facts before you move into action. As noted in Chapter 20, "Apply Logical Thinking When You Experience Uncertainty," whenever you face a situation that calls for a decision or an action, remember to sort everything you know about it into three buckets: (a) what you are sure of (with the reasons that you are sure), (b) what you believe but are not yet sure of, and (c) what you don't have

a clue about. Based on those classifications, decide whether you need more facts. Be clear in how you express yourself in conversation, indicating if you are certain based on facts or are only speculating based on what you believe or have inferred from prior experiences. To expand your understanding, pay special attention to at least two things that differ from your opinion or experience every day.

4. **Focus on the needs of the people who are dependent on your work.** Your work is always used by someone else to do something else. Regardless of what you do, your aim is to help others do their work. The benefits of focusing on other people's needs are unlimited, for example:

   - It radically increases the likelihood that you will be perceived as a valuable colleague.
   - It improves your understanding of other people and their needs, which builds your ability to influence them.
   - It makes your work more meaningful and interesting— even the most mundane tasks become honorable and hence enjoyable since they are important for others.

How to Inculcate and Monitor These Behaviors in Your Team

Here are some things to consider:

1. Use the approach I described in Chapter 31, "Develop Your People into Stars." The weekly personal and development goal, for example, could be focused on these four behaviors.
2. As my client Barbara did, create a team contract in which these thought patterns or behaviors are described. All team members should sign it. Then have a professional graphic

designer turn it into a poster and display it prominently in your workplace.

3. Use the four behaviors as a basis for individual development plans, development goals, and development talks with your team members.

4. Design a team barometer that covers the four behaviors, plus any other issues that relate to your team's well-being and performance. The barometer results can be the basis of team discussions, individual development, and personal reflections.

5. Set aside ten to fifteen minutes at the end of team meetings to discuss and reflect upon the behaviors displayed. Were all four behaviors modeled?

Adopt a Recruiting Practice to Enable Diversity and Selection of the Right People

Demanding to implement in your work life

How do you embrace diversity when you recruit people to your team or organization? By being fact based.

First, you need to cultivate a deep understanding of the true requirements for success in the position you are hiring for. I find that most companies and leaders have a far too shallow understanding of that, which opens up the entire recruiting process—from where they source potential candidates, whom they choose to interview, what data they acquire around each candidate, how they set up the interviews, to whom they hire—to ambiguity. Knowing in detail what success in the position looks like, both short- and long-term, including the specific skills and personal attributes that are critical, is decisive.

Second, you need to collect the right information about each candidate, particularly their character. A candidate should have good skills and knowledge, but the candidate's character— integrity, track record in self-improvement, core behaviors, true motives, and so on—is just as important. Hiring a competent person with bad character is worse than hiring an incompetent person with a good character, since it can erode the culture of the workplace. Competence is much easier to build than character.

The following process for recruiting a person to your team or organization will strengthen your ability to assess and hire the right people, including dealing with any biases that could hinder diversity.

Interestingly, most of the candidates that have interviewed with my clients said that this process is among the most interesting and professional they have experienced, which has given my clients a boost in their employee branding.

First, Answer Three Questions About the Job

Like everything in life, true insight comes with effort. Detailing the true requirements of a position you need to fill is no exception. To do this well, take a pen and a piece of paper and answer the following questions. Your answers will make it easy to create clarity and focus throughout recruiting—from designing the job ad to selecting the right candidate.

1. What does success look like in this position? What are the tangible and measurable outcomes of a successful candidate? For example:
   - After four weeks in the position?
   - After three months in the position?
   - After one year in the position?
2. What are the barriers and challenges a candidate needs to overcome to be successful in each of the time horizons above? For example:

   To execute better on current plans and objectives. Describe why the execution needs to improve, why it has not been good, and how it can be improved.

   To develop and implement new plans and objectives. Describe the new plans and objectives, why they are needed, and what will be challenging in developing and implementing them.

To improve existing methods and approaches to meet new or current objectives. Describe the methods and approaches, why they need to be improved, and how that can be approached.

To develop and implement new methods and approaches to meet new or current objectives. Describe the new methods and approaches, why they need to be developed, and how they can be successfully implemented.

To rally troops and stakeholders around plans, objectives, methods, and approaches. Describe what troops and stakeholders need to be rallied, the specific roles they must play, what will be challenging to rally them, and how that could be achieved.

3. What specific and testable skills in each of the following three dimensions are required for a candidate to overcome those barriers and challenges? Here you should use the descriptions of the three basic skill categories, problem-solving, managing, and people development, from Chapter 31, "Develop Your People into Stars." Select the level you think is required in each of the subcategories of these skill categories and explain in writing why it is required.

When you have reasonably detailed answers to these questions, you have made a great investment in launching a successful recruiting process.

To Assess the Candidate's Character, Assess Their Mental Maturity

Before we go through the actual recruiting process, let's say a few words about assessing a candidate's most important attribute—character.

As human beings, we all must master and navigate three worlds:

- Our inner world: what goes on inside of us—thoughts, feelings, and needs.
- Our outer world: all the contexts that we are members of; for example, work, family, and friends.
- And lastly, the world that connects the inner and outer worlds.

Within each of these worlds are conflicts that engender ambiguity and uncertainty, attributes that humans have a hard time dealing with, as we thrive on clarity, control, and predictability. To manage these ever-present challenges and be productive and successful, we must evolve.

In my experience, most adults fail to do this. Instead of evolving, they tend to simply override or discard the conflicting needs within and between these worlds and hence have only a partial connection to reality. As a result, their explanations and claims for what happened or what is happening can range from incomplete to utterly absurd.

What does this mean for hiring? When you assess candidates for a position, you can get a sense of their character or mental maturity by probing their approach to responsibility and the integrity and completeness with which they explain conflicts or challenges in their current and past work contexts.

Designing Your Process

Request information from your candidate in writing. Reading what people write is a more effective way to understand their thinking patterns, motives, and other capabilities than engaging with them face-to-face, especially if you have not mastered the skill of disassociating yourself and observing what a person really does and says. Simply reading their words allows you to form impressions that are unbiased by whatever irrational influences may occur in an interview; moreover, it allows you to prepare for the eventual interview more effectively, as you will have a better idea of what questions to focus on.

Ask candidates to *not* attach photos to their résumés. This is important. If they do it anyway, beware. They have most likely figured out that their appearance, rather than their performance, has been an asset to them—or alternatively, they can't understand a simple instruction, lack attention to detail, or want to do things their own way.

Research shows that we tend to view people we find good-looking as smarter; unless you are choosing models for a fashion show, hiring should never be a beauty contest. With no photo, you can't subconsciously form an opinion about the person before you've engaged with the person's thinking.

Finally, request that candidates write about each of the following topics.

The Position They Hope to Fill

To be confident that a candidate has the right experience and skills for a position, you should let the candidate elaborate on the position based on a description of the critical accomplishments required. Here is a template I have used with clients. You can adjust it for your specific position.

For a person to be successful in the position as marketing specialist for product areas A, B, and C, three critical accomplishments are required during the first twelve months.

Description of Accomplishment 1: For product areas A and B, coordination among product managers, sales, and marketing needs to be tangibly improved. These departments tend to come together far too late and face challenges in agreeing on a coordinated plan for product launches, marketing messages, channel selection, quarterly customer events, and exhibitions. In your position as the marketing specialist, you are expected to initiate and lead the efforts to improve the situation.

1. What are your initial ideas about the root causes behind the current situation, based on your experience and other sources of insight?

2. What key performance indicators or other tangible indicators would you use to measure progress toward the needed improvements in twelve months?

3. What would your personal and professional challenges be and your sources of discomfort in pursuing the needed improvements?

4. How would you design an overall plan to achieve this improvement? What are its key steps or phases?

5. What measurable work results and accomplishments could you produce three months into your plan?

The candidates' answers will give you reliable insights into their ability to think as well as execute, set goals, and monitor their progress. You'll also get a robust view of their past experiences in dealing with similar issues. And since this example also involves the skill to lead people and create cooperation across departments, you would get a solid view of their capabilities in this decisive skill set.

The Candidate Should Elaborate on Past Failures and Successes

To get insight into candidates' true character, ask them to thoroughly reflect in writing on their past failures and successes. Here is a template I have used with clients that you can adapt (the questions for probing successes are similar):

Describe two of your past professional failures.
Failure one: Describe what you were trying to achieve, in which context, as well as how you would define the failure.
1. What was your specific role and responsibility in pursuing what you wanted to achieve?
2. What other people were involved and what were their specific roles and responsibilities?
3. How would you describe the root causes behind the failure; for example, who did/did not do what, how, and why?
4. What would you do differently today if you were pursuing the same objective?

Answers will reveal the candidates' character, level of self-awareness, and ability to take responsibility for failures as well as successes.

Preparing and Designing the Interview

The perspectives you gain on the candidates from their written responses will determine how you spin each interview. Use this summary template to prepare:

Insights on the candidate's answers to questions about the required accomplishments in the position.	
What are the major gaps in the candidate's answers?	What questions could I ask to probe deeper into these gaps?
Insights on the candidate's answers in dealing with past failures and successes.	
What are the major gaps in the candidate's answers?	What questions could I ask to probe deeper into these gaps?

Here are some things to think about when conducting the interviews:

- Does what the candidate says fit with their observable behavior in the conversation?
- Based on their observed behaviors, what seem to be the candidate's true motives?
- Is the candidate dedicated to everyday personal and professional growth and development?
- Is the candidate shying away from the subject matter at hand? If so, ask why.
- Is the candidate willing to take responsibility for their actions and outcomes?
- Don't be charmed. Think of charm as an intentional behavior, not a personality trait.

- Is the candidate too transparent, giving away too many details too soon? When people are not honest, what they say often does not sound credible to themselves even if it does to you, so they keep talking. If the candidate seems to talk too much, always ask yourself why.

- Bring up issues and ideas that you know are controversial (and even stupid), issues and ideas that should stimulate debate. If you don't get any pushback on your ideas, it's a red flag. Also, analyze the questions the candidates ask about your business, the problems you are facing, and the role for which you are hiring. What does it tell you about their interests and competence? Also check how ambitious they are; how many of your problems can they help you solve at the same time?

- Promises are cheap, especially when they are unsolicited. If a candidate makes promises when you have not asked for any, ask yourself why. The reason may be that the candidate is picking up on doubts you have that you might not be aware of yourself.

- Just because a candidate works for one of the great companies in your industry, it does not mean that the candidate is great.

Some other things to keep in mind: People are less likely to lie about themselves when they are asked straightforward questions. And people seldom volunteer information about themselves that makes them look worse. So blunt questions about a candidate's demonstrated reliability, integrity, and dependability are always a good investment, no matter how awkward they may be to ask.

Use Scenarios

A good and fun way to get to know candidates is to engage them in work scenarios. Here are some examples from a client of mine who was hiring for the position of global product manager:

Scenario 1. You launch a new product that had excellent performance during testing and has shown to be clearly better than what is available in the market. However, the reception from internal salespeople has been lukewarm. How would you handle that situation and turn it around?

Scenario 2. A challenge with Research & Development in our company is that they give a long lead time on completion of projects, as they strive for perfection. But getting to perfection conflicts with the optimal time to market. How would you address this issue?

Scenario 3. You are managing a product assortment where 20 percent of the offering is bringing in 80 percent of the sales. However, the sales team is strongly pushing to keep the rest of the assortment as it covers gaps and offers potential to increase sales, and some items are parts of key contracts, et cetera. You are also launching a new family of products that will add to the assortment. How would you deal with this?

Scenario 4. The sales team has been negotiating a multimillion-dollar, multiyear tender with a customer. The customer has reviewed the proposal and has come back asking for a further 5 percent discount on unit price. The required profit margins are there even with the discount. Will you approve it? If not, how would you make it work?

Scenario 5. You have a product family offering that has sold quite well over the years and established a strong reputation. Now you are launching a new product family that is proving to be much better in trials. Keeping both families in the offering would make the assortment too big and inventories would increase a lot. How will you go about phasing out the old assortment and phasing in the new one?

Conducting the Interview

Interviewing a candidate for a job is not a popularity contest. It is a high-stakes real-work situation that has an element of stress and pressure built in. You must do three things in particular:

Make the candidate stick to the subject! Make sure the person you are interviewing sticks to the subjects you are discussing and answers all your questions. Be aware of the most challenging and uncomfortable things you need to ask and ask them directly. How the candidate deals with them can tell you a lot.

Not sticking to the subject matter could have other serious implications beyond the candidate being weak in dealing with awkward questions; it could be a sign that the candidate doesn't understand what you're talking about. This in turn could be a sign that the person is not used to taking in information or understanding things beyond past experiences, or that you have not explained the subject matter or the question clearly enough.

Make the candidate take responsibility! You need to probe the candidate's natural orientation to take responsibility as opposed to viewing others as responsible for the problems that will inevitably arise. The easiest way to do this is to ask about the candidate's earlier failures as well as successes. Ask the person to simply describe the situation when he or she experienced a serious failure: What was it? What was the goal that was not achieved? Who was involved? What were the people's roles and responsibilities? In chronological order, what happened? Who did what and why? And so on. The candidate's answers—or nonanswers—will give you a good idea about how the person embraces responsibility, as well as assigns responsibility outside himself or herself. Every sign of an inadequate sense of responsibility should elicit further probing.

Adjust your tone properly! You need to be open to changing your tone and temperament when you engage with the candidate. It is utterly meaningless to stay friendly and warm if the person you interview is giving you a lot of crap thoughts or explanations, or diverging from the subject matter. A simple comment or question like "I hear what you are saying, but I can't understand what that has to do with what we are talking about. Can you explain why you aren't talking about what we are supposed to be talking about?" This is not meant to be offensive, just refreshingly straightforward.

Final Words:
Thoughts on Selecting a Good Place to Work

I have given you proven tools and principles to help you master the most important environment there is: your inner environment—that is, your mind. When you master your mind, you can unlock your intrinsic motivation, which will enable you to reach any goal and achieve things you did not think you were capable of.

As you have noticed, I have not mentioned the importance of the workplace in the book. Why? There are at least three reasons for that.

First, your workplace will not matter, even if it is a great one, if you don't master your mind to unlocking your intrinsic motivation.

Second, at the end of the day, you are the only person who is able look out for your best interest and to shape your own destiny.

Third, a great workplace can change into a bad one in an instant. Creating an excellent work environment with great behaviors, values, and ways of working takes immense time, dedicated effort, and constant attention, but it takes very little time and effort to destroy it. Just hiring one bad leader in a great workplace is enough to cause serious damage, not only for that department but for all other departments in the company. I have seen so many examples of this that I have lost count.

So, what should you do? Stop caring about where you work or whether it is a good or bad workplace? Absolutely not. A good workplace is important because it makes it easier for you to enjoy going to work, invest the time and effort necessary to engross yourself in your work, and to think good, positive thoughts about your work when you are not there.

But what should you look for in a workplace to judge whether it is good or bad? The answer is in *how well the workplace is designed to enable its people to experience a sense of autonomy*—in other words, the workplace is designed in a way that enables you to feel that you can influence, shape, and grow in your own work.

My mentor, Csikszentmihalyi, made an interesting discovery when he measured how frequently people experience flow in their lives. Even though people experience flow more frequently in their work life than in any other area in their lives, they often feel the least satisfied with their work life compared to the other areas. Why? When we discussed this, Csikszentmihalyi's view was that the most likely reason was that work itself is viewed by people as something they must do, *not something they choose to do*. In addition, in most big organizations the work and tasks are already predefined and are constantly influenced by forces beyond people's own zone of influence; for example, decisions made by top management.

Obviously, it is impossible to create perfect autonomy in any organization, but companies can do a better or a worse job to enable their people to experience a healthy level of autonomy.

There are four areas you should investigate to understand whether a company you are interested in is doing better or worse in enabling their people to experience autonomy. Write down as many questions you can come up with for each of the four areas below. Ask yourself how you can get answers to your questions in a smart way. Reading annual reports and articles in the media about the company is good, but the best way to make your investigation is to engage with people familiar with the company, either current or former employees. To increase the reliability of the answers to your questions, simply make sure to talk with more than one person familiar with the company. Instead, talk to three or four people unrelated to each other.

Here are the four areas you should investigate:

The level of decentralized decision-making and planning in the company. The more decisions and ownership over departmental planning a leader has, the more freedom they can potentially give to their people in how they in turn plan and decide over their own work. An understanding of which decisions are taken on what level, how, when, and by whom in the company, gives a good indication for how top-down things are executed in the company. The rule of thumb is: *The more top-down, the lower sense of autonomy among the people.*

When you engage with people from the company, ask them about how decision-making is made. Try to understand the annual cycle of business planning and goal-setting in the company. Is it done entirely top-down or in a way where people on lower levels in the organization actively and tangibly impact and influence whatever is decided as priorities and goals at the top of the house?

The size of the staff functions and their "interference" with the business. The idea behind staff functions is that they should support and advise the line organization, that is, the people who operate the business. Examples of common staff functions are human resources, legal, finance/accounting, public relations, and technology/IT.

The bigger the staff functions are, the more interference they cause in the line organization, which in turn impacts the sense of autonomy of the people operating the business. Big staff functions generally launch multiple central initiatives every year that the line organization needs to spend time on implementing. Most of these central initiatives are either irrelevant since the people who came up with them lack any deeper insight into the true nature of the business or are driven in a way that just causes frustration or confusion in the line organization.

So, when you do analyze a company, try to get a sense of the size of the staff functions, their track record of launching central initiatives, and the overall sentiment in the line organization around the staff functions and their value add.

The quality and robustness of collaboration between people and departments. Few things lower the sense of autonomy more than being dependent on other people with whom collaboration is not working well. In my experience, poor collaboration in companies is a universal problem and causes major issues in company performance as well as in employee satisfaction.

When you engage with people familiar with the company you are interested in, ask questions about collaboration: How well is collaboration between people and departments working? What do the company and its leaders do to secure great collaboration? What are the main reasons when collaboration fails? What are the company's collaboration issues, and how do they solve them? What are the consequences for people refusing to collaborate successfully with others?

In my experience, people who do not collaborate well are seldom dealt with. At best they are moved to another part of the organization in the hope that they will improve how they collaborate (which they most often fail to do).

Fairness, frequency, and robustness in assessing individual performance and development needs. The company's assessment of how you perform and how you need to develop in your job is extremely important for your sense of autonomy.

To understand how well the company is doing in this area, you should ask people familiar with it questions such as: How does the company establish truly clear goals and expectations on what an employee should deliver and how they should develop during a given time frame, for example during a month, a quarter, or a year? Are these goals and expectations described in a way that enables (1) the development of a clear plan to pursue them, (2) continuous monitoring of progress, and (3) a clear and unambiguous assessment on whether they are met or not at the end of the stipulated time frame? How is the dialogue set up between the employees and their boss to continuously monitor progress and engage in feedback and coaching to secure progress? How is the assessment done at the end of the stipulated time frame? What are the consequences for employees not meeting their goals?

Related to this is also the leaders' focus on actively *delegating their tasks as development opportunities for their people*. Strive to ask questions about how leaders go about delegating their tasks. Does it happen at all? If so, how often does it happen? What is the thinking behind who the leader delegates a task to? What is the success rate in how the delegated tasks are performed?

Spend sufficient time investigating these areas (as well as other areas important to you) to understand whether or not the company you are interested in offers a good workplace.

But please remember: The workplace will not matter, even if it is a great one, if you don't master your mind to unlock your intrinsic motivation for all types of work tasks.

PS: Do you wonder if I still play the piano? Yes I do, for one to two hours every day. I still enjoy it as much as I did when I was a kid. As much as I love music for itself, I am even more grateful that it led me to find the keys to my intrinsic motivation, which I have used throughout my life, in everything I have been involved in.

I hope you can feel similarly inspired about your own work, and that my book has shown you a path.

Must-Reads

Barking Up the Wrong Tree: The Surprising Science Behind Why Everything You Know About Success Is (Mostly) Wrong by Eric Barker

Before You Know It: The Unconscious Reasons We Do What We Do by John Bargh

Building Expertise: Cognitive Methods for Training and Performance Improvement by Ruth C. Clark

Creativity: Flow and the Psychology of Discovery and Invention by Mihaly Csikszentmihalyi

Deep Work: Rules for Focused Success in a Distracted World by Cal Newport

Drive: The Surprising Truth About What Motivates Us by Daniel H. Pink

Fearless: The Undaunted Courage and Ultimate Sacrifice of Navy SEAL Team SIX Operator Adam Brown by Eric Blehm

Finding Flow: The Psychology of Engagement with Everyday Life by Mihaly Csikszentmihalyi

Getting Things Done: The Art of Stress-Free Productivity by David Allen

Handbook of Psychodiagnostic Testing: Analysis of Personality in the Psychological Report by Henry Kellerman and Anthony Burry

Honorable Work: A Process for Achieving Success & Satisfaction in Your Work by Tim Anstett

Influence: Science and Practice by Robert B. Cialdini

Interview Math: Over 50 Problems and Solutions for Quant Case Interview Questions by Lewis C. Lin

Lifting Depression: A Neuroscientist's Hands-On Approach to Activating Your Brain's Healing Power by Kelly Lambert

Mind-Brain-Gene: Toward Psychotherapy Integration by John Arden

Mindshift: Break Through Obstacles to Learning and Discover Your Hidden Potential by Barbara Oakley

Misbehaving: The Making of Behavioral Economics by Richard H. Thaler

Peak: Secrets from the New Science of Expertise by Anders Ericsson and Robert Pool

Principles: Life and Work by Ray Dalio

Systems of Denial: Strategic Resistance to Military Innovation by Andrew Hill and Stephen J. Gerras

The Corrosion of Character: The Personal Consequences of Work in the New Capitalism by Richard Sennett

The Evolving Self: A Psychology for the Third Millennium by Mihaly Csikszentmihalyi

The Inner Game of Work: Focus, Learning, Pleasure, and Mobility in the Workplace by W. Timothy Gallwey

The Power of Habit: Why We Do What We Do and How to Change by Charles Duhigg

The Pyramid Principle: Logic in Writing and Thinking by Barbara Minto

The Will to Lead: Running a Business with a Network of Leaders by Marvin Bower

"Thinking Critically About Critical Thinking: A Fundamental Guide for Strategic Leaders" by Stephen J. Gerras

True Professionalism: The Courage to Care About Your People, Your Clients, and Your Career by David H. Maister

Notes

3: Use If-Then "Implementation Intentions"

1. Peter M. Gollwitzer, "Implementation Intentions: Strong Effects of Simple Plans," *American Psychologist,* July 1999, www.researchgate.net/publication /232586066_Implementation_Intentions_Strong_Effects_of_Simple_Plans.

5: Learn like the Terminator

1. https://dictionary.apa.org/confirmation-bias.
2. For more information, see Barbara Oakley's site at https://barbaraoakley.com/.

7: Commit to Daily Journaling

1. See Giada Di Stefano, Gary P. Pisano, Francesca Gina, and Bradley R. Staats, "Making Experience Count: The Role of Reflection in Individual Learning," Harvard Business School NOM Unit Working Paper No. 14–093, *SSRN,* March 26, 2014, https://papers.ssrn.com/sol3/papers.cfm?abstract_id =2414478.
2. John B. Arden, *Mind-Brain-Gene: Toward Psychotherapy Integration* (New York: W. W. Norton, 2019).

8: Visit Your "Green Zone" Every Day

1. Ron Friedman, "Why Too Much Data Disables Your Decision Making," *Psychology Today,* December 4, 2012.

Section Two: Shape Your Destiny: Evolve Your Mindset to Become the Superstar You Can Be

1. Alia J. Crum and Ellen J. Langer, "Mind-Set Matters: Exercise and the Placebo Effect," *Psychological Science* 18, no. 2 (2007): 165–71, https://dash.harvard.edu /bitstream/handle/1/3196007/Langer_ExcersisePlaceboEffect.pdf?sequence=1.
2. Cara Feinberg, "The Mindfulness Chronicles," *Harvard Magazine,* September–October 2010, https://harvardmagazine.com/2010/09/the-mindfulness-chronicles.
3. Tim Minchin's speech is viewable at www.youtube.com/watch?v=yoEezZD71sc.

20: Apply Logical Thinking When You Experience Uncertainty

1. Hilary Jacobs Hendel, "Ignoring Your Emotions Is Bad for Your Health. Here's What to Do About It," *Time,* February 27, 2018, https://time.com/5163576 /ignoring-your-emotions-bad-for-your-health/.

23: Limit Your Time on Social Media

1. Nicholas Carr, "How Smartphones Hijack Our Minds," *Wall Street Journal,* October 6, 2017, www.wsj.com/articles/how-smartphones-hijack-our-minds -1507307811.
2. Russell B. Clayton, Glen Leshner, and Anthony Almond, "The Extended iSelf: The Impact of iPhone Separation on Cognition, Emotion, and Physiology," *Journal of Computer-Mediated Communication,* January 8, 2015, https: //onlinelibrary.wiley.com/doi/full/10.1111/jcc4.12109.
3. Adrian F. Ward, Kristen Duke, Ayelet Gneezy, and Maarten W. Bos, "Brain Drain: The Mere Presence of One's Own Smartphone Reduces Available Cognitive Capacity," *Journal of the Association for Consumer Research,* April 2017, https://doi.org/10.1086/691462.
4. Andew K. Przybylski and Netta Weinstein, "Can You Connect with Me Now? How the Presence of Mobile Communication Technology Influences Face-to-Face Conversation Quality," *Journal of Social and Personal Relationships,* July 19, 2012, https://doi.org/10.11772F0265407512453827.

26: Cultivate a Mindset for Inner Peace

1. Douglas Robson, "For Rafael Nadal, Self-Doubt Can Be Good for His Game," *USA Today,* November 10, 2013, https://www.usatoday.com/story/sports/tennis /2013/11/10/rafael-nadal-ends-season-no-1-ranking/3489567/.
2. www.businessinsider.com/ray-dalio-interview-henry-blodget-1-2017.
3. Jaime Rocca and Sara Wilde, *The Connector Manager* (London: Virgin Books, 2019).

Section Three: Master the Second-Biggest Obstacle for Professional Success and Well-Being: Other People

1. Eric Barker, *Barking Up the Wrong Tree: The Surprising Science Behind Why Everything You Know About Success Is (Mostly) Wrong* (New York: HarperOne, 2017).

29: Make It Easy for People to Follow Your Advice and to View You as a Thought Leader

1. For more detail on how people with a superficial understanding often are overconfident, see the research on the Dunning-Kruger effect. For example, Justin Kruger and David Dunning, "Unskilled and Unaware of It: How Difficulties in Recognizing One's Own Incompetence Lead to Inflated Self-Assessments," *Journal of Personality and Social Psychology,* 1999, https://psycnet.apa.org /record/1999-15054-002?doi=1.

30: Don't Avoid Difficult People, Embrace Them

1. John Bargh, *Before You Know It: The Unconscious Reasons We Do What We Do* (New York: Atria Books, 2018).

Index